Best of Country Pies

Get Ready to Roll Out Some of The Best Pies in the Country!

COOKS ACROSS THE COUNTRY put lots of love into homemade pies...probably because there's a lot to love about these down-home pastries. Just what makes them so popular? When it comes to pies, the possibilities are limitless!

Fruit-laden pies fresh from the oven...pies filled with from-scratch custard or pudding cooked on the stovetop...cool and creamy pies chilled in the refrigerator...frosty ice cream and freezer pies...crumbly crisps and cobblers that don't require a crust...and scrumptious tarts tailored to singles or a crowd. We have them all in this *Best of Country Pies* cookbook—and more!

There are 229 pleasing pie recipes packed into the pages of this book. It's chock-full of the most-requested pie recipes from past issues of *Taste of Home* and its "sister" publications. You can make these recipes with confidence because each and every one is a tried-and-true favorite of a fellow cook's family. Our test kitchen staff prepared and taste-tasted each pie as well, selecting it for a book we call "The Best". We've included full-color photos of most pies, so you can see what they look like before you start baking.

Before you roll up your sleeves and bring out the rolling pin, though, turn to the Pie Pointers chapter on page 4. There you'll find step-by-step instructions with photos on how to roll out the perfect pastry and how to create decorative crusts. You'll also learn the secret to making magnificent meringues. Whether you're a beginner or a well-seasoned baker, you're sure to appreciate these easy-to-follow techniques and the handy tips we've sprinkled throughout the rest of the book.

Mastering the art of baking pies is simply a matter of a little know-how and a lot of practice. You'll get just that with the 229 pie recipes compiled in this convenient collection you're sure to turn to again and again!

Makes a Great Gift!

To order additional copies of the *Best of Country Pies* book, specify item number 31528 and send $15.99 (plus $3.95 shipping/insured delivery for one book, $4.50 for two or more) to: Country Store, Suite 4761, P.O. Box 990, Greendale WI 53129-0990. To order by credit card, call toll-free 1-800/558-1013 or visit our Web site at *www.reimanpub.com*.

Pictured on front cover: Berry Cream Pie (p. 23); pictured on previous page: Apple Blackberry Pie (p. 22); pictured on back cover: Golden Peach Pie (p. 16).

Best of Country Pies

Editor: Jean Steiner
Art Director: Niki Malmberg
Food Editor: Janaan Cunningham
Associate Food Editors: Coleen Martin, Diane Werner
Senior Recipe Editor: Sue A. Jurack
Associate Editors: Julie Schnittka, Heidi Reuter Lloyd
Food Photography: Rob Hagen, Dan Roberts
Food Photography Artists: Stephanie Marchese, Vicky Marie Moseley
Photo Studio Manager: Anne Schimmel
Production: Ellen Lloyd, Catherine Fletcher
Publisher: Roy Reiman

© 2001 Reiman Publications, LLC
5400 S. 60th St., Greendale WI 53129
International Standard Book Number: 0-89821-323-1
Library of Congress Control Number: 2001135765
Printed in USA.

Pie Pointers

WHETHER you're a beginner or well-seasoned cook, you'll appreciate this chapter's practical pointers for baking pies. You'll learn how to make and shape pie pastry (get started using the two simple recipes below)…create decorative cursts…whip up magnificent meringues…and more!

Pastry for Single-Crust Pie

When rolling out the pie pastry, mend any cracks by wetting your fingers and pressing the dough together.

1-1/4 cups all-purpose flour
1/2 teaspoon salt
1/3 cup shortening
4 to 5 tablespoons cold water

In a bowl, combine flour and salt; cut in the shortening until crumbly. Gradually add water, tossing with a fork until a ball forms. Roll out pastry to fit a 9-in. or 10-in. pie plate. Transfer pastry to pie plate. Trim pastry to 1/2 in. beyond edge of pie plate; flute edges. Fill or bake shell according to recipe directions. **Yield:** 1 pastry shell (9 or 10 inches).

Pastry for Double-Crust Pie

This recipe is also used when preparing a lattice-topped pie (see how on page 7).

2 cups all-purpose flour
3/4 teaspoon salt
2/3 cup shortening
6 to 7 tablespoons cold water

In a bowl, combine flour and salt; cut in the shortening until crumbly. Gradually add water, tossing with a fork until dough forms a ball. Divide dough in half so that one ball is slightly larger than the other. Roll out larger ball to fit a 9-in. or 10-in. pie plate. Transfer pastry to pie plate. Trim pastry even with edge. Pour desired filling into crust. Roll out second ball; Position over filling; cut slits in pastry. Trim pastry to 1 in. beyond edge of pie plate. Fold top crust over bottom crust. Flute edges. Bake according to recipe directions. **Yield:** pastry for double-crust pie (9 or 10 inches).

Preparing Perfect Pie Pastry

● Classic pie pastry recipes are prepared with solid shortening. Lard or butter-flavored shortening can be substituted for plain shortening if desired.

● Measure all ingredients carefully for best results.

● Combine flour and salt thoroughly before adding the shortening and water.

● Use ice-cold water to make pastry dough. Add only enough water, a tablespoon at a time, to moisten the flour mixture. The amount of water will vary due to weather conditions.

● The key to producing a flaky crust is to avoid overmixing once you start adding the ice-cold water to the flour and shortening mixture.

● Roll out pastry with as little additional flour as possible for more tender crusts. A pastry cloth and rolling pin cover will make the job easier without using excess flour. Roll the dough to a circle about 2 inches larger than the pie plate and ease into the pie plate. Don't stretch the pastry to fit because that will make the bottom crust shrink while the pie is baking.

● Chill pie pastry dough 30 minutes before rolling to make it easier to handle.

● Select glass or dull-finished aluminum pie plates for crisp golden crusts. Shiny pans produce a soggy crust.

● Because of the high fat content in a pastry, do not grease the pie plate unless the recipe directs.

Making and Shaping Pie Pastry

1 Accurately measure flour and salt and combine in a large bowl. Using a pastry blender or two knives, cut the shortening into the dry ingredients until crumbly and the pieces are the size of small peas.

2 Sprinkle flour mixture with ice water, a tablespoon at a time, and gently mix with a fork until the flour mixture is moist enough to hold together. The amount of water needed will vary from day to day, depending on the humidity in the air.

3 Gently shape the mixture into a single ball if preparing the single-crust pastry. If preparing the pastry for a double-crust pie, divide the dough in half so that one half is slightly larger (the larger half will be used for the bottom crust and the smaller piece will be used for the top crust or lattice top).

Lightly flour the working surface and flatten the pastry balls, pressing together any cracks or breaks.

At this point, many cooks wrap the dough in plastic wrap and refrigerate for 30 minutes. This resting time makes it easier to roll out the dough.

4 Lightly coat your working surface with all-purpose flour before rolling out the ball of dough.

Rub flour over the rolling pin; begin rolling the flattened ball from the center of the dough and move toward the edges. Roll out dough evenly to a circle about 2 in. larger than the pie plate and 1/8 in. thick.

5 To easily lift the delicate pastry to the pie plate, roll it up onto the rolling pin. Position over the edge of the pie plate and unroll. Let the pastry ease into the plate; do not stretch the pastry to fit. Add the filling. Trim the pastry with a kitchen shears or sharp knife (1/2 in. beyond plate edge for a single-crust pie, or trim edges even with pie plate for a double-crust pie). For a single-crust pie, fold the 1/2-in. edge of pastry under and flute.

6 For a double-crust pie, roll out the smaller second ball into a 12-in. circle that is 1/8 in. thick. Roll pastry up onto the rolling pin; position over filling. Cut several steam vents or slits in the center of the dough.

7 Using your kitchen shears or knife, trim top crust to 1 in. beyond plate edge. Fold top crust over bottom crust. Turn to page 7 for decorative crust techniques.

1

2

3

4

5

6

7

Creating Decorative Crusts
Is Easy as Pie!

A FOLD here, a twist there—with some simple but snappy finger work, you can turn out a pie that's as yummy to look at as it is to eat.

Eye-catching edges, cutout pieces of pastry trimming an otherwise plain upper crust and well-woven lattice tops all give pie crusts fancy finishing touches. And although they may look difficult, often these tasty decorations are easy to complete.

To help unravel the mystery behind making such appealing crusts, we've compiled simple-to-follow instructions on time-tested treatments, so you can create your own at home.

Go ahead and roll out any of these beauties today. Your cutting-edge wizardry will surely earn a host of compliments from family and friends!

Before you create any of the decorative edges shown on these two pages, you'll have to trim the dough so you have the right amount for an attractive edge. The edges can't be formed without enough dough—but too much will result in a thick edge that will lose its shape during baking.

Most of the treatments shown here require a built-up edge or a rolled edge. The pastry should be trimmed to 1/2 in. beyond the rim of the pie plate for a single-crust pie and 1 in. for a double-crust pie. This overhang is then turned under to form the built-up edge.

The other kind of edge, a flat edge, is made simply by trimming the pastry even with the edge of the pie plate.

(Keep in mind that the terms "rolled edge" and "flat edge" describe how the dough should be trimmed before the decorative edges are made.)

Now, embellish those edges with one of these fancy trims.

Ruffle Edge (below) is suitable for a single- or double-crust pie.

Make a rolled edge. Position your thumb and index finger about 1 in. apart on the edge of the crust, pointing out.

Position the index finger on your other hand between the two fingers and gently push the pastry toward the center in an upward direction. Continue around the edge.

Rope Edge (below) is suitable for a single- or double-crust pie.

Make a rolled edge. Then make a fist with one hand and press your thumb at an angle into the dough. Pinch some of the dough between your thumb and index finger.

Repeat at about 1/2-in. intervals around the crust. For a looser-looking rope, position your thumb at a wider angle and repeat at 1-in. intervals.

Cut Scalloped Edge (below) is suitable for a single-crust pie.

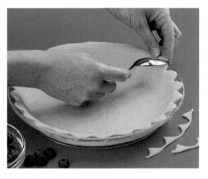

Make a flat edge. Hold a teaspoon or tablespoon upside down and roll the tip of the spoon around the edge of the pastry, cutting it. Remove and discard the cut pieces to create a scalloped look.

Remember—the larger the spoon, the bigger the scallops.

Braided Edge (below) is suitable for a single-crust pie. Make enough pastry for a double crust.

Line a 9-in. pie plate with the bottom crust and shape a flat edge.

Roll remaining dough into a 10-in. x 8-in. rectangle. With a sharp knife, cut twelve 1/4-in.-wide strips. Gently braid three strips of dough. Brush edge of pastry with water. Place braid on edge of crust and press lightly to secure.

Repeat with remaining strips, attaching additional braids until entire edge is covered. Use foil to protect the edges from over-browning.

Leaf Trim (below) is suitable for a single-crust pie.

Make enough pastry for a dou-

ble crust. Line a 9-in. pie plate with the bottom crust and make a flat edge. Roll out remaining dough to 1/8-in. thickness.

Cut out leaf shapes, using 1-in. to 1-1/2-in. cookie cutters. With a sharp knife, score dough to create leaf veins. Brush bottom of each leaf with water.

Place one or two layers of leaves around the pastry edge. Press lightly to secure. Use foil to protect the edges from over-browning.

You can also use this technique with other cookie cutter designs, such as stars, hearts and apples. Vary them to suit the special occasion or season you are celebrating.

Lattice Top (above right) is suitable for a double-crust pie. Line a 9-in. pie plate with the bottom crust and trim pastry to 1 in. beyond edge of plate.

Roll out remaining dough into a 12-in. circle. With a fluted pastry wheel, pizza cutter or sharp knife, cut dough into 1/2-in.- to 1-in.-wide strips. Lay strips in rows about 1/2 in. to 3/4 in. apart.

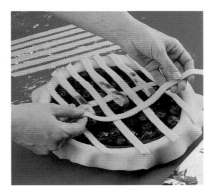

(Use longer strips for the center of the pie and shorter strips for the sides.)

Fold every other strip halfway back. Starting at the center, add strips at right angles, lifting every other strip as the cross strips are put down. Continue to add strips, lifting and weaving until lattice top is completed.

Trim strips even with pastry edge. Fold bottom crust up and over ends of strips. Finish by making a ruffle, rope or fluted edge.

Pastry Cutouts (below) are suitable for a single- or double-crust pie.

To make cutouts, roll out dough to 1/8-in. thickness. Cut

out with 1-in. to 1-1/2-in. cookie cutters of desired shape. With a sharp knife, score designs (if desired) on cutouts.

For a single-crust pie, bake cutouts on an ungreased baking sheet at 400° for 6-8 minutes or until golden brown. Remove to wire rack to cool. Arrange over cooled filling on baked pie.

For a double-crust pie, brush bottom of each unbaked cutout with water and arrange over top crust of an unbaked pie. Press lightly to secure. Bake pie according to recipe.

Fluted Edge (below) is suitable for a single- or double-crust pie.

Make a rolled edge. Position your index finger on the edge of the crust, pointing out. Place the thumb and index finger of your other hand on the outside edge and pinch dough around the index finger to form a V shape. Continue around the edge.

As you can see, a decorative edge will lend an upper-crust look to any down-home dessert. In no time, you'll be able to bake up a picture-perfect pie that just might be too pretty to slice!

Optional Finishing Touches

• For a sparkling top crust, lightly brush with water and sprinkle with 1 tablespoon sugar just before baking.

• In a hurry? Finish crust edges quickly by trimming the pastry even with pie plate and pressing the tines of a fork around the edge. Dip the fork tines in flour often to keep them from sticking to the pastry.

Making Crumb Crusts

WHY RELY on store-bought crumb crusts when you can easily prepare a better-tasting version from scratch?

In a mixing bowl, combine crumbs, sugar and melted butter or margarine; blend well. Press the mixture onto the bottom and up the sides of an un-greased 9-in. pie plate. Chill 30 minutes before filling or bake at 375° for 8-10 minutes or until crust is lightly browned. Cool before filling.

To enjoy a crisp crust, serve pies prepared with graham cracker crusts the same day they are made. Frozen ice cream pies are the exception.

Type of Crust	Amount of Crumbs	Sugar	Butter *or* Margarine, melted
Graham Cracker	1-1/2 cups (24 squares)	1/4 cup	1/3 cup
Chocolate Wafer	1-1/4 cups (20 wafers)	1/4 cup	1/4 cup
Vanilla Wafer	1-1/2 cups (30 wafers)	none	1/4 cup
Cream-Filled Chocolate	1-1/2 cups (15 cookies)	none	1/4 cup
Gingersnap	1-1/2 cups (24 cookies)	none	1/4 cup
Macaroon Cookie	1-1/2 cups	none	1/4 cup
Pretzel (grease pie pan)	1-1/4 cups	1/4 cup	1/2 cup

Making Crumbs

Place cookies or crackers in a heavy-duty resealable plastic bag. Seal bag, pushing out as much air as possible. Press a rolling pin over the bag, crushing the crackers to fine crumbs. Crumbs can also be made in a blender or food processor according to the manufacturer's directions.

Prebaking Pie Shells

DRIED uncooked beans or uncooked rice can be used like pie weights to weigh down a crust when it's prebaked. The beans or rice prevent the sides of the pie crust from shrinking and slipping down the pie plate during baking.

To give this technique a try, just follow the directions below. But first, prick the unbaked pastry shell with a fork to keep the pastry from bubbling as it bakes.

There is no need to throw out the beans or rice. While we don't recommend using them in recipes, you can save them to use as pie weights again and again.

1. Line the pastry shell with a double thickness of heavy-duty foil. Fill it with 1-1/2 cups of dried beans or rice. Bake at 450° for 8 minutes.

2. With oven mitts, carefully remove the foil and beans from the pie crust. Continue baking until the crust is golden brown, about 5-6 minutes.

Technique Foils Burned Crusts

YOU'VE rolled out a tender pie crust from scratch and filled it to the brim with a scrumptious filling. So once it's in the oven, you don't want the edges becoming too dark—or worse yet, burning.

That's a common concern. Pie crust edges often brown before the rest of the pie. But a little cover-up can help, especially if the pie has to bake longer than 30 minutes.

How do you go about creating such a thing? Our handy home economists have cooked up this easy method (shown at right) to shield those deliciously flaky edges:

Fold a 12-in. square of foil into quarters. Place the folded corner toward you. Measure 3-3/4 in. up each adjacent side and cut out an arc joining the two sides. Discard the center.

Unfold the remaining foil and place it over the un-baked pie. Gently crimp the foil around the edges of the crust to secure. Bake for 20 to 30 minutes before removing the foil.

If you prefer, you can use the foil shield during the final 10 to 20 minutes of baking if the edges are browning too quickly.

Your picture-perfect pie will be ready to slice and savor!

Magnificent Meringues

WHIPPING UP meringue isn't difficult, but it does require some time and attention to details. These pointers from the American Egg Board will help you make, serve and store meringues with ease:

● Since humidity is the most critical factor in making a successful meringue, choose a dry day. Meringues can absorb moisture on a humid day and become limp and sticky.

● The temperature of the eggs is important if egg whites are to reach their greatest volume. Eggs separate most cleanly when they are cold. After separating, place the whites in a mixing bowl and let stand at room temperature for 20-30 minutes.

● For the greatest volume, place whites in a small clean metal or glass mixing bowl. Even a drop of fat from the egg yolk or a film of oil sometimes found on plastic bowls will prevent egg whites from foaming. For this reason, be sure to use clean beaters.

● Adding cream of tartar (or another acidic ingredient) before beating the whites is important—it stabilizes the egg white foam.

● After stiff peaks form (whites will look glossy and have tips that stand straight without bending), check that the sugar is dissolved. It will feel silky smooth when rubbed between your thumb and index finger.

● Spread the meringue over hot filling to minimize "weeping", the watery layer between the meringue and filling.

● Use a metal spatula to seal the meringue to edges of pastry. This will help prevent shrinkage while baking.

● Cool the pie away from drafts at room temperature for 1 hour, then refrigerate at least 3 hours before serving. Leftovers need to be stored in the refrigerator.

1. Combine egg whites and cream of tartar in a mixing bowl. Beat on medium speed until large white foamy bubbles form, about 1 minute.

2. Add sugar 1 tablespoon at a time, beating on high just until stiff glossy peaks form and the mixture is silky smooth, about 3 minutes.

3. Use a metal spatula to spread meringue over hot filling. Be sure to seal meringue to edges of pastry to prevent shrinkage while baking.

p. 12

p. 18

p. 16

p. 13

p. 22

Fresh Fruit Pies

CHOCK-FULL OF FRUIT. Clockwise from upper left: Glazed Raspberry Pie (p. 12), Deep-Dish Blackberry Pie (p. 18), Golden Peach Pie (p. 16), Apple Blackberry Pie (p. 22) and Candy Apple Pie (p. 13).

Cheddar Pear Pie

Cynthia LaBree, Elmer, New Jersey

I take this pie to lots of different gatherings, and I make sure to have copies of the recipe with me since people always ask for it.

    4 large ripe pears, peeled and thinly sliced
1/3 cup sugar
    1 tablespoon cornstarch
1/8 teaspoon salt
    1 unbaked pastry shell (9 inches)
TOPPING:
    1/2 cup shredded cheddar cheese
    1/2 cup all-purpose flour
    1/4 cup butter *or* margarine, melted
    1/4 cup sugar
    1/4 teaspoon salt

In a bowl, combine pears, sugar, cornstarch and salt. Pour into pastry shell. Combine topping ingredients until crumbly; sprinkle over the filling. Bake at 425° for 25-35 minutes or until crust is golden and cheese is melted. Cool on a wire rack for 15-20 minutes. Serve warm. Store in the refrigerator. **Yield:** 6-8 servings.

Glazed Raspberry Pie

Gillian Batchelor, Crescent Valley, British Columbia

(Pictured below and on p. 10)

This recipe has been copied for countless people over the years. There's no mistaking that raspberries give this tall pie its good looks and divine flavor.

    5 cups fresh raspberries, *divided*
    1 cup water, *divided*
    1 cup sugar
    3 tablespoons cornstarch
    2 tablespoons lemon juice
    1 package (3 ounces) cream cheese, softened

    1 tablespoon butter *or* margarine, softened
    1 tablespoon milk
    1 pastry shell (9 inches), baked
Fresh mint, optional

In a saucepan, combine 2/3 cup raspberries and 2/3 cup water. Simmer, uncovered, for 3 minutes. Strain raspberries and discard seeds; set juice aside. In another saucepan, combine sugar, cornstarch and remaining water until smooth. Add raspberry juice. Bring to a boil over medium heat; cook and stir for 2 minutes or until thickened. Remove from the heat; stir in lemon juice. Cool. In a small mixing bowl, beat cream cheese, butter and milk until smooth. Spread onto the bottom and up the sides of pastry shell. Fill pastry shell with the remaining raspberries. Slowly pour glaze over berries. Refrigerate until serving. Garnish with mint if desired. **Yield:** 6-8 servings.

Cranberry Cherry Pie

Marilyn Williams, Matthews, North Carolina

(Pictured above)

Guests won't know how quickly you made this sweet-tart pie. It starts with convenient canned pie filling.

    3/4 cup sugar
    2 tablespoons cornstarch
    1 can (21 ounces) cherry pie filling
    2 cups cranberries
Pastry for double-crust pie (9 inches)
Milk and additional sugar

In a bowl, combine sugar and cornstarch. Stir in pie filling and cranberries. Line a 9-in. pie plate with bottom pastry; trim to 1 in. beyond edge of plate. Pour filling into crust. Roll out remaining pastry to fit top of pie. Cut slits in pastry or cut out stars with a star-shaped cookie cutter. Place pastry over filling; trim, seal and flute edges. Arrange star cutouts on pastry. Brush with milk and sprinkle with sugar. Cover edges loosely with foil. Bake at 375° for 55-60 minutes or until crust is golden brown and filling is bubbly. Cool on a wire rack. **Yield:** 6-8 servings.

Candy Apple Pie

Cindy Kleweno, Burlington, Colorado

(Pictured below and on p. 10)

Like a combination of apple and pecan pie, this sweet treat usually tops off our holiday meals.

- 6 cups thinly sliced peeled tart apples
- 2 tablespoons lime juice
- 3/4 cup sugar
- 1/4 cup all-purpose flour
- 1/2 teaspoon ground cinnamon *or* nutmeg
- 1/4 teaspoon salt

Pastry for double-crust pie (9 inches)
- 2 tablespoons butter *or* margarine

TOPPING:
- 1/4 cup butter *or* margarine
- 1/2 cup packed brown sugar
- 2 tablespoons whipping cream
- 1/2 cup chopped pecans

In a bowl, toss apples with lime juice. Combine dry ingredients; add to apples and toss. Line a 9-in. pie plate with bottom pastry; trim to 1 in. beyond edge of pie plate. Add filling; dot with butter. Roll out remaining pastry to fit top of pie; place over filling. Trim, seal and flute edges high. Cut slits in top. Bake at 400° for 40-45 minutes or until golden and apples are tender. Meanwhile, melt butter in a small saucepan. Stir in brown sugar and cream; bring to a boil, stirring constantly. Remove from heat and stir in pecans. Pour over top crust. Bake 3-4 minutes more or until bubbly. Serve warm. **Yield:** 8 servings.

Harvest Pie

Roberta Murren, Overbrook, Kansas

There's a cornucopia of fall flavor baked into this eye-pleasing fruit pie. Even my husband, who says he isn't a cranberry fan, loves it. By using frozen berries, I can make it year-round.

- 2 cans (8 ounces *each*) crushed pineapple
- 1 package (12 ounces) fresh *or* frozen cranberries, chopped
- 1 cup packed brown sugar
- 1/2 cup sugar
- 3 tablespoons all-purpose flour
- 2 tablespoons butter *or* margarine
- 3/4 cup chopped walnuts *or* pecans
- 1/2 teaspoon almond extract, optional
- 1/4 teaspoon salt

Pastry for double-crust pie (9 inches)

Drain pineapple, reserving 1/4 cup juice. Set pineapple aside. In a saucepan, combine the cranberries, sugars and pineapple juice. Bring to a boil; cook and stir for 5 minutes. Combine flour and pineapple; add to cranberry mixture. Cook and stir over medium heat until mixture comes to a boil; cook and stir for 2 minutes or until thickened. Remove from the heat; stir in the butter, nuts, almond extract if desired and salt. Cool. Line a 9-in. pie plate with bottom pastry; trim to 1 in. beyond edge of pie plate. Add filling. Roll out remaining pastry to fit top of pie; place over filling. Trim, seal and flute edges. Cut slits in top. Bake at 400° for 40-45 minutes or until golden brown. Cool on a wire rack. **Yield:** 6-8 servings.

Fall Pear Pie

Ken Churches, San Andreas, California

(Pictured above)

A wide slice of this festive fruity pie is a great end to a delicious meal. The mellow flavor of pears is a refreshing alternative to the more common pies for the holidays.

    8 cups thinly sliced peeled pears
    3/4 cup sugar
    1/4 cup quick-cooking tapioca
    1/4 teaspoon ground nutmeg
Pastry for double-crust pie (9 inches)
    1 egg, lightly beaten
    1/4 cup whipping cream, optional

In a large bowl, combine pears, sugar, tapioca and nutmeg; let stand for 15 minutes. Line a 9-in. pie plate with bottom crust; add pear mixture. Roll out remaining pastry to fit top of pie. Place over filling; seal and flute edges. Cut large slits in top; brush with egg. Bake at 375° for 55-60 minutes or until the pears are tender. Cool on a wire rack. Pour cream through slits if desired. Store in the refrigerator. **Yield:** 8 servings.

Golden Apricot Pie

Jo Martin, Patterson, California

This pie is pretty as a picture and "absolutely apricot" in flavor, with the fruit's beautiful golden-orange color showing through its lattice top.

    2 packages (6 ounces *each*) dried apricots
2-3/4 cups water
Pastry for double-crust pie (9 inches)
    1 cup sugar
    3 tablespoons cornstarch

    1/8 teaspoon nutmeg
    1 tablespoon butter *or* margarine

In a saucepan, combine apricots and water; bring to a boil. Reduce heat and simmer for 20-22 minutes. Remove from the heat; cool. Line a 9-in. pie plate with bottom crust. Drain apricots, reserving 3/4 cup liquid. Arrange apricots in pie shell. Combine sugar, cornstarch, nutmeg and reserved apricot liquid until smooth. Pour over apricots; dot with butter. Make a lattice crust. Trim, seal and flute edges. Bake at 400° for 50-55 minutes or until crust is golden brown and filling is bubbly. Cool on a wire rack. **Yield:** 8 servings.

Strawberry-Rhubarb Crumb Pie

Paula Phillips, East Winthrop, Maine

(Pictured below)

Everyone seems to have a rhubarb patch here in Maine. This pie won first prize at our church fair. I hope it's a winner at your house, too!

    1 cup sugar
    2 tablespoons all-purpose flour
    1 egg
    1 teaspoon vanilla extract
    3/4 pound fresh rhubarb, cut into 1/2-inch
        pieces (about 3 cups)
    1 pint fresh strawberries, halved
    1 unbaked pastry shell (9 inches)
TOPPING:
    3/4 cup all-purpose flour
    1/2 cup packed brown sugar
    1/2 cup quick-cooking *or* rolled oats
    1/2 cup cold butter *or* margarine

In a mixing bowl, beat the sugar, flour, egg and vanilla; mix well. Gently fold in rhubarb and strawberries. Pour into pie shell. For topping, combine flour, brown sugar and oats in a small bowl; cut in butter until crumbly. Sprinkle over fruit. Bake at 400° for 10 minutes. Reduce heat to 350°; bake 35 minutes longer or until crust is golden brown and filling is bubbly. Cool on a wire rack. Store in the refrigerator. **Yield:** 8 servings.

Giant Pineapple Turnover

Carolyn Kyzer, Alexander, Arkansas

Fresh apple, canned pineapple and plump raisins combine in this fun turnover. The crust, made from refrigerated pie pastry, is a tasty shortcut.

- 1 **sheet refrigerated pie pastry**
- 1 **medium tart apple, peeled and coarsely chopped**
- 1 **can (8 ounces) crushed pineapple, well drained**
- 3/4 **cup sugar**
- 1/3 **cup finely chopped celery**
- 1/3 **cup raisins**
- 1/3 **cup chopped walnuts**
- 1/4 **cup all-purpose flour**

Ice cream, optional

Unfold pastry and place on a baking sheet. In a bowl, combine the apple, pineapple, sugar, celery, raisins, walnuts and flour; toss gently. Spoon filling over half of crust to within 1 in. of edge. Fold pastry over filling and seal edges well. Cut slits in top. Bake at 400° for 30-35 minutes or until crust is golden brown and filling is bubbly. Cool on a wire rack. Cut into wedges. Serve with ice cream if desired. **Yield:** 4 servings.

Cherry Almond Pie

Ramona Pleva, Lincoln Park, New Jersey

(Pictured above)

I grew up in northern Michigan, where three generations of my family have been cherry producers. This traditional cherry pie makes a mouth-watering dessert.

- 4 **cups pitted canned *or* frozen tart red cherries**
- 3/4 **cup sugar**
- 1 **tablespoon butter *or* margarine**

Pinch salt

- 1/4 **cup cornstarch**
- 1/3 **cup cold water**
- 1/4 **teaspoon almond extract**
- 1/4 **teaspoon red food coloring, optional**

Pastry for double-crust pie (9 inches)

Drain cherries, reserving 2/3 cup juice in a saucepan; discard remaining juice. To the juice, add cherries, sugar, butter and salt. In a small bowl, combine cornstarch and water until smooth; stir into cherry mixture. Bring to a boil over medium heat. Cook and stir for 2 minutes or until thickened and bubbly. Remove from the heat; stir in the almond extract and food coloring if desired. Cool. Line a 9-in. pie plate with bottom pastry; add filling. Make a lattice crust. Trim, seal and flute edges. Bake at 375° for 45-50 minutes or until crust is golden brown and filling is bubbly. Cool on a wire rack. **Yield:** 6-8 servings.

Measuring Frozen Rhubarb

When using frozen rhubarb, measure it frozen, then thaw completely. Drain in a colander, but do not press liquid out.

Golden Peach Pie

Shirley Olson, Polson, Montana

(Pictured below and on p. 10)

Fifteen years ago, I entered this beautiful pie in the Park County Fair in Livingston. It won a first-place blue ribbon plus a purple ribbon for "Best All Around"! My large family—six children and 14 grandchildren— and many friends all agree with the contest judges that it's very delicious.

Pastry for double-crust pie (9 inches)
- 1 cup sugar
- 1/4 cup cornstarch
- 1/4 teaspoon ground nutmeg
- 1/8 teaspoon salt
- 2 teaspoons lemon juice
- 1/2 teaspoon grated orange peel
- 1/8 teaspoon almond extract
- 5 cups sliced peeled fresh peaches (about 5 medium)
- 2 tablespoons butter *or* margarine

Milk

Line a 9-in. pie plate with bottom pastry; trim even with edge of plate. Set aside. In a bowl, combine sugar, cornstarch, nutmeg and salt; stir in lemon juice, orange peel and extract. Add the peaches; toss gently. Pour into crust; dot with butter. Roll out remaining pastry to fit top of pie; make decorative cutouts in pastry. Set cutouts aside. Place top crust over filling. Trim, seal and flute edges. Brush pastry and cutouts with milk; place cutouts on top of pie. Cover the edges loosely with foil. Bake at 400° for 40 minutes. Remove foil; bake 10-15 minutes longer or until crust is golden brown and filling is bubbly. Cool on a wire rack. **Yield:** 6-8 servings.

Banana Streusel Pie

Gayle Kuipers, Holland, Michigan

(Pictured above)

I obtained this recipe from my mom, who everyone considers a great cook. It's been in the family for a number of years. We usually serve it at holiday meals, and it's always a crowd-pleaser.

- 1 unbaked pastry shell (9 inches)
- 1/4 cup sugar
- 1/2 teaspoon ground cinnamon
- 1 teaspoon cornstarch
- 1/2 cup pineapple juice
- 2 tablespoons lemon juice
- 1-1/2 teaspoons grated lemon peel
- 4 cups sliced firm bananas (5 to 6 medium)

STREUSEL:
- 1/2 cup all-purpose flour
- 1/2 cup packed brown sugar
- 1/3 cup chopped macadamia nuts *or* almonds
- 1 teaspoon ground cinnamon
- 1/4 cup cold butter *or* margarine

Line the unpricked pastry shell with a double thickness of foil. Bake at 450° for 10 minutes. Remove the foil and bake 2 minutes more or until pastry is golden brown; set aside. Reduce heat to 375°. In a saucepan, combine the sugar, cinnamon and cornstarch. Add the pineapple juice, lemon juice and peel; mix well. Bring to a boil. Cook and stir for 1-2 minutes or until thickened and bubbly. Remove from the heat. Fold in bananas; pour into crust. For streusel, combine flour, brown sugar, nuts and cinnamon; cut in butter until the mixture resembles coarse crumbs. Sprinkle over the filling. Cover edges of pie with foil. Bake at 375° for 40 minutes or until topping is golden brown and filling is bubbly. Cool on a wire rack. **Yield:** 6-8 servings.

Ruby Grape Pie

Fred Smeds, Reedley, California

Having a 75-acre vineyard, my wife, Paula, and I use grapes in a lot of different recipes from salads to desserts. This one calling for seedless red grapes is an unusual and tasty pie. We hope you enjoy it as much as we do.

- 4 cups halved seedless red grapes (about 2 pounds)
- 2/3 cup sugar
- 1/2 teaspoon ground cinnamon
- 3 tablespoons cornstarch
- 2 tablespoons lemon juice
- 1 tablespoon grated lemon peel
- Pastry for double-crust pie (9 inches)
- 2 tablespoons butter *or* margarine

In a saucepan, combine grapes, sugar and cinnamon; toss to coat. Let stand for 15 minutes. Combine cornstarch, lemon juice and peel; stir into grape mixture. Bring to a boil; cook and stir for 2 minutes or until thickened. Line a 9-in. pie plate with bottom crust. Pour grape mixture into crust. Dot with butter. Roll out remaining pastry to fit top of pie; place over filling. Trim, seal and flute edges; cut slits in top. Cover edges loosely with foil. Bake at 425° for 20 minutes. Reduce heat to 350°; remove foil and bake 30-35 minutes longer or until the crust is golden brown and filling is bubbly. Cool on a wire rack. **Yield:** 6-8 servings.

Dutch Apricot Pie

Joanne Hutmacher, Lemoore, California

I freeze several bagfuls of apricots when they are in season, thinking of this pie all the while. At holiday time, there's nothing like a luscious taste of summer. The crunchy toasted pecans in the topping make this dessert extra special.

- 3/4 cup sugar
- 2 tablespoons quick-cooking tapioca
- 4 cups sliced fresh apricots (about 16)
- 1 tablespoon lemon juice
- Pastry for single-crust pie (9 inches)
- TOPPING:
- 2/3 cup all-purpose flour
- 1/2 cup sugar
- 1/2 cup chopped pecans, toasted
- 1/4 cup butter *or* margarine, melted

In a bowl, combine sugar and tapioca; mix well. Add apricots and lemon juice; toss to coat. Let stand for 15 minutes. Line a 9-in. pie plate with pastry. Trim pastry to 1/2 in. beyond edge of plate; flute edges. Pour filling into crust. In a small bowl, combine flour, sugar and pecans. Stir in butter. Sprinkle over filling. Cover edges loosely with foil. Bake at 350° for 15 minutes. Remove foil; bake 25-30 minutes longer or until crust is golden

brown and filling is bubbly. Cool on a wire rack. Store in the refrigerator. **Yield:** 6-8 servings.

Summer Berry Pie

Judi Messina, Coeur d'Alene, Idaho

(Pictured below)

Mom puts luscious fresh blueberries, strawberries and raspberries to great use in this cool, refreshing pie. A super dessert on a hot day, it provides a nice light ending to a hearty meal.

- 1-1/2 cups sugar
- 6 tablespoons cornstarch
- 3 cups cold water
- 1 package (6 ounces) raspberry *or* strawberry gelatin
- 2 cups fresh blueberries
- 2 cups sliced fresh strawberries
- 2 cups fresh raspberries
- 2 graham cracker crusts (9 inches)
- 4 cups whipped topping
- Fresh mint and additional sliced strawberries

In a large saucepan, combine sugar, cornstarch and water until smooth. Bring to a boil; cook and stir for 2 minutes or until thickened. Remove from the heat. Stir in gelatin until dissolved. Refrigerate for 15-20 minutes or until mixture begins to thicken. Stir in the blueberries, strawberries and raspberries. Pour into crusts and chill until set. Garnish with whipped topping, mint and strawberries. **Yield:** 2 pies (6-8 servings each).

Deep-Dish Blackberry Pie

Dorothy Lilliquist, Brooklyn Center, Minnesota

(Pictured below and on p. 10)

For years whenever I went home to visit, my mom brought up jars of canned blackberries from the cellar and treated us to this delicious pie.

> 3 cups fresh *or* frozen blackberries, thawed and drained
> 1/2 cup sugar
> 2 tablespoons cornstarch
> 1 teaspoon lemon juice
> 1/4 teaspoon ground cinnamon
> **TOPPING:**
> 3/4 cup all-purpose flour
> 3 teaspoons sugar, *divided*
> 1/4 teaspoon salt
> 3 tablespoons cold butter *or* margarine
> 1 tablespoon shortening
> 3 tablespoons cold water
> 1 egg white, beaten

Place blackberries in a bowl. Combine sugar and cornstarch; sprinkle over berries. Add lemon juice and cinnamon; toss to coat. Spoon into a greased 1-qt. baking dish. In a bowl, combine the flour, 1 teaspoon sugar and salt. Cut in butter and shortening until mixture resembles coarse crumbs. Add water; toss with a fork until a ball forms. Roll out pastry; make a lattice crust. Crimp edges. Brush with egg white; sprinkle with remaining sugar. Bake at 375° for 40-45 minutes or until crust is golden brown and filling is bubbly. Cool on a wire rack. **Yield:** 2 servings. **Editor's Note:** Instead of a lattice crust, pastry can be rolled out to fit top of dish. Cut slits in pastry; place over berries. Trim, seal and flute edges.

Apple Meringue Pie

Virginia Kraus, Pocahontas, Illinois

(Pictured above)

I received this recipe from my mother-in-law, and it's one of my husband's favorites. It's a nice variation on traditional apple pie.

> 7 cups thinly sliced peeled tart apples
> 2 tablespoons lemon juice
> 2/3 cup sugar
> 2 tablespoons all-purpose flour
> 1/3 cup milk
> 2 egg yolks, beaten
> 1 teaspoon grated lemon peel
> **Pastry for single-crust pie (9 inches)**
> 1 tablespoon butter *or* margarine, cubed
> **MERINGUE:**
> 3 egg whites
> 1/4 teaspoon cream of tartar
> 6 tablespoons sugar

In a large bowl, toss apples with lemon juice. In a small bowl, whisk sugar, flour, milk, egg yolks and lemon peel until smooth. Pour over apples and toss to coat. Line a 9-in. pie plate with pastry; trim to 1/2 in. beyond edge of pie plate and flute edges. Pour filling into crust; dot with butter. Cover edges loosely with foil. Bake at 400° for 20 minutes. Remove foil; bake 25-30 minutes longer or until apples are tender. Reduce heat to 350°. In a mixing bowl, beat the egg whites and cream of tartar on medium speed until foamy. Gradually beat in sugar, 1 tablespoon at a time, on high just until stiff glossy peaks form and sugar is dissolved. Spread evenly over hot filling, sealing edges to crust. Bake for 15 minutes or until golden brown. Cool on a wire rack for 1 hour. Store in the refrigerator. **Yield:** 6-8 servings.

Sky-High Strawberry Pie

Janet Mooberry, Peoria, Illinois

(Pictured above)

This pie is my specialty. It's fairly simple to make but so dramatic to serve. The ultimate taste of spring, this luscious pie has a big, fresh berry taste. I've had many requests to bring it to gatherings.

    3 quarts fresh strawberries, *divided*
1-1/2 cups sugar
    6 tablespoons cornstarch
  2/3 cup water
Red food coloring, optional
    1 deep-dish pastry shell (10 inches), baked
    1 cup whipping cream
1-1/2 tablespoons instant vanilla pudding mix

In a large bowl, mash enough berries to measure 3 cups. In a saucepan, combine the sugar and cornstarch. Stir in the mashed berries and water; mix well. Bring to a boil over medium heat, stirring constantly. Cook and stir for 2 minutes. Remove from the heat; add food coloring if desired. Pour into a large bowl. Chill for 20 minutes, stirring occasionally, until mixture is just slightly warm. Fold in the remaining berries. Spoon into pie shell. Chill for 2-3 hours. In a small mixing bowl, whip cream until soft peaks form. Sprinkle pudding mix over cream and whip until stiff. Garnish pie with cream mixture. **Yield:** 8-10 servings.

Berry Big Pie

Janelle Seward, Ontario, Oregon

I take this giant fruit pie to almost every potluck dinner I'm invited to. It's always well-received. The crust is

so easy to make, and we have lots of berries on hand since they grow here on our small acreage. With a dessert this size, everyone can enjoy a luscious piece.

    4 cups all-purpose flour
    1 tablespoon sugar
    2 teaspoons salt
1-3/4 cups shortening
  1/2 cup cold water
    1 egg
    1 tablespoon white vinegar
FILLING:
    8 cups fresh *or* frozen blackberries*
    2 cups sugar
  1/2 cup all-purpose flour
Half-and-half cream

In a large bowl, combine flour, sugar and salt; cut in shortening until mixture resembles coarse crumbs. In a bowl, combine the water, egg and vinegar; stir into flour mixture just until moistened. Form into a log. Cover and refrigerate for 1 hour. On a floured surface, roll out two-thirds of the dough into an 18-in. x 14-in. rectangle. Carefully press onto the bottom and up the sides of a 13-in. x 9-in. x 2-in. baking dish. Combine the blackberries, sugar and flour; pour into crust. Roll out remaining dough; make a lattice crust. Crimp edges. Brush pastry with cream. Bake at 400° for 15 minutes; reduce heat to 350°. Bake about 1 hour longer or until crust is golden brown and filling is bubbly. Cool completely on a wire rack. Store in the refrigerator. **Yield:** 12-16 servings. ***Editor's Note:** If using frozen blackberries, do not thaw before making the filling.

Festive Fruit Pie

Dorothy Smith, El Dorado, Arkansas

Fresh banana slices, canned pineapple tidbits and chopped pecans dress up the cherry filling in this fuss-free, festive-looking pie. For even quicker results, you can substitute a prepared graham cracker crust for the baked pastry shell.

    1 cup sugar
  1/4 cup all-purpose flour
    1 can (21 ounces) cherry pie filling
    1 can (14 ounces) pineapple tidbits, drained
    1 package (3 ounces) orange gelatin
    3 to 4 medium firm bananas, sliced
    1 cup chopped pecans
    2 pastry shells, baked (9 inches)
Whipped topping, optional

In a large saucepan, combine the sugar and flour. Stir in the cherry pie filling and pineapple tidbits. Bring to a boil over medium heat; cook and stir for 2 minutes or until thickened and bubbly. Remove from the heat; stir in the orange gelatin until dissolved. Set aside to cool. Gently stir in the sliced bananas and pecans. Pour into pastry shells. Refrigerate for at least 3 hours. Garnish with whipped topping if desired. **Yield:** 2 pies (6-8 servings each).

Chocolate Raspberry Pie

Ruth Bartel, Morris, Manitoba

(Pictured below)

After tasting this pie at my sister-in-law's house, I had to have the recipe. I love the chocolate and raspberry layers separated by a dreamy cream layer. It's a joy to serve this standout treat.

- 1 unbaked pastry shell (9 inches)
- 3 tablespoons sugar
- 1 tablespoon cornstarch
- 2 cups fresh *or* frozen unsweetened raspberries, thawed

FILLING:
- 1 package (8 ounces) cream cheese, softened
- 1/3 cup sugar
- 1/2 teaspoon vanilla extract
- 1/2 cup whipping cream, whipped

TOPPING:
- 2 squares (1 ounce *each*) semisweet chocolate
- 3 tablespoons butter (no substitutes)

Line unpricked pastry shell with a double thickness of heavy-duty foil. Bake at 450° for 8 minutes. Remove foil; bake 5 minutes longer. Cool on a wire rack. In a saucepan, combine sugar and cornstarch. Stir in the raspberries; bring to a boil over medium heat. Boil and stir for 2 minutes. Remove from the heat; cool for 15 minutes. Spread into shell; refrigerate. In a mixing bowl, beat cream cheese, sugar and vanilla until fluffy. Fold in whipped cream. Carefully spread over raspberry layer. Cover and refrigerate for at least 1 hour. Melt chocolate and butter; cool for 4-5 minutes. Pour over filling. Cover and chill for at least 2 hours. Store in the refrigerator. **Yield:** 6-8 servings.

Fresh Blueberry Pie

Linda Kerman, Mason, Michigan

(Pictured above)

I've been making this dessert for over 30 years. It represents our state well because Michigan is the leader in blueberry production.

- 3/4 cup sugar
- 3 tablespoons cornstarch
- 1/8 teaspoon salt
- 1/4 cup cold water
- 5 cups fresh blueberries, *divided*
- 1 tablespoon butter *or* margarine
- 1 tablespoon lemon juice
- 1 pastry shell (9 inches), baked

In a saucepan over medium heat, combine sugar, cornstarch, salt and water until smooth. Add 3 cups blueberries. Bring to a boil; cook and stir for 2 minutes or until thickened and bubbly. Remove from the heat. Add butter, lemon juice and remaining berries; stir until butter is melted. Cool. Pour into the pastry shell. Refrigerate until serving. **Yield:** 6-8 servings.

Purple Plum Pie

Michelle Beran, Claflin, Kansas

I can never resist a tart, tempting slice of this beautiful pie. It's a down-home dessert that makes any meal special. This pie is a terrific way to put bountiful summer plums to use. And no one can guess how easy it is to prepare.

- 4 cups sliced fresh plums (about 1-1/2 pounds)
- 1/2 cup sugar
- 1/4 cup all-purpose flour

1/4 teaspoon salt
1/4 teaspoon ground cinnamon
1 tablespoon lemon juice
1 unbaked deep-dish pastry shell (9 inches)
TOPPING:
1/2 cup sugar
1/2 cup all-purpose flour
1/4 teaspoon ground cinnamon
1/4 teaspoon ground nutmeg
3 tablespoons cold butter *or* margarine

In a bowl, combine the plums, sugar, flour, salt, cinnamon and lemon juice; pour into the pastry shell. For topping, combine sugar, flour, cinnamon and nutmeg in a small bowl; cut in butter until the mixture resembles coarse crumbs. Sprinkle over filling. Bake at 375° for 50-60 minutes or until crust is golden brown and filling is bubbly. Cover edges of crust during the last 20 minutes to prevent overbrowning. Cool on a wire rack. **Yield:** 8 servings.

Apple Custard Pie

Carol Adams, Medina, Texas

One of my favorite ways to use apples is in this pie. There is no need to pull out your rolling pin to make this treat—it has an easy press-in crust under a mouthwatering filling.

1-1/2 cups all-purpose flour
1/2 teaspoon salt
1/2 cup cold butter *or* margarine
3 cups sliced peeled tart apples
1/3 cup sugar
1 teaspoon ground cinnamon
CUSTARD:
1 cup evaporated milk

1 egg
1/2 cup sugar

In a bowl, combine flour and salt; cut in butter until crumbly. Press onto the bottom and up the sides of a 9-in. pie plate. Arrange apples over the crust. Combine sugar and cinnamon; sprinkle over apples. Bake at 375° for 20 minutes. For custard, whisk milk, egg and sugar until smooth; pour over apples. Bake 25-30 minutes longer or until a knife inserted near the center comes out clean. Cool on a wire rack for 1 hour. Store in the refrigerator. **Yield:** 6-8 servings.

Mom's Peach Pie

Sally Holbrook, Pasadena, California

(Pictured below)

A delightful summertime pie, this dessert is overflowing with fresh peach flavor. Each sweet slice is packed with old-fashioned appeal. The streusel topping makes this pie a little different than the ordinary.

1 egg white
1 unbaked pastry shell (9 inches)
3/4 cup all-purpose flour
1/2 cup packed brown sugar
1/3 cup sugar
1/4 cup cold butter *or* margarine
6 cups sliced peeled fresh peaches

Beat egg white until foamy; brush over the bottom and sides of the pastry. In a small bowl, combine flour and sugars; cut in butter until mixture resembles fine crumbs. Sprinkle two-thirds over the pastry; top with peaches. Sprinkle with remaining crumb mixture. Bake at 375° for 40-45 minutes or until filling is bubbly and peaches are tender. Cool on a wire rack. **Yield:** 6-8 servings.

1/4 cup all-purpose flour
2 teaspoons lemon juice
1/8 teaspoon salt
1 unbaked pastry shell (9 inches)
STREUSEL:
1/2 cup quick-cooking oats
1/2 cup packed brown sugar
1/4 cup all-purpose flour
1/4 cup cold butter *or* margarine

Squeeze the end of each grape opposite the stem to separate skins from pulp. Set skins aside. Place pulp in a saucepan; bring to a boil. Boil and stir for 1 minute. Press through a strainer or food mill to remove seeds. Combine pulp, skins, sugar, flour, lemon juice and salt; pour into pastry shell. Combine oats, brown sugar and flour; cut in butter until mixture resembles coarse crumbs. Sprinkle over filling. Cover edges loosely with foil. Bake at 425° for 15 minutes. Remove foil; bake 20 minutes longer or until golden brown. Cool on a wire rack. **Yield:** 8 servings.

Apple Blackberry Pie

Dorian Lucas, Corning, California

(Pictured below and on p. 10)

After a blackberry-picking trip, my husband and I decided to include a few in an apple pie we were making. It was the best we'd ever tasted! We live near the mountains with our two children. Ingredients for fruit pies grow all around us.

2 cups all-purpose flour
1 teaspoon sugar
1 teaspoon salt
1 teaspoon ground cinnamon
2/3 cup cold butter *or* margarine
4 to 6 tablespoons cold water

Bonnie Blue-Barb Pie

Andrea Holcomb, Torrington, Connecticut

(Pictured above)

Rhubarb and blueberries are both native to our area, and this pie combines the flavors beautifully. We are fortunate to have a healthy rhubarb patch in our garden. It keeps us supplied with rhubarb from spring until well into fall.

1-1/2 cups fresh *or* frozen rhubarb, cut into
1/2-inch pieces
1-1/2 cups fresh *or* frozen blueberries
1 cup sugar
1/4 cup all-purpose flour
1/4 teaspoon salt
Pastry for double-crust pie (9 inches)
2 tablespoons butter *or* margarine

In a large bowl, combine rhubarb and blueberries. Combine sugar, flour and salt. Sprinkle over the fruit; toss lightly. Line a 9-in. pie plate with pastry; add filling. Dot with butter. Make a lattice crust. Trim, seal and flute edges. Bake at 450° for 10 minutes. Reduce heat to 350°; bake 35 minutes longer or until crust is golden brown and filling is bubbly. Cool on a wire rack. **Yield:** 8 servings. **Editor's Note:** If using frozen fruit, thaw and drain well.

Concord Grape Pie

Linda Erickson, Harborcreek, Pennsylvania

My husband, Jim, and I grow 235 acres of Concords a few miles from Lake Erie. We're rewarded by a crop with a distinctive, robust flavor, perfect for this scrumptious pie, which is our favorite harvesttime dessert. We savor every forkful.

4-1/2 cups Concord grapes (2 pounds)
1 cup sugar

FILLING:

- 5 cups thinly sliced peeled tart apples (about 6 medium)
- 1 cup fresh blackberries
- 1/2 cup packed brown sugar
- 4-1/2 teaspoons cornstarch
- 1 teaspoon ground cinnamon
- 1 teaspoon ground nutmeg

In a bowl, combine the flour, sugar, salt and cinnamon; cut in butter until crumbly. Gradually add water, tossing with a fork until dough forms a ball. Divide dough in half. Roll out one portion to fit a 9-in. pie plate; place pastry in plate and trim even with edge. In a bowl, combine apples and blackberries. Combine the brown sugar, cornstarch, cinnamon and nutmeg; add to fruit mixture and toss to coat. Pour into crust. Roll out remaining pastry to fit top of pie; place over filling. Trim, seal and flute edges. Cut slits in pastry. Add decorative cutouts if desired. Cover edges loosely with foil. Bake at 450° for 10 minutes. Reduce heat to 350°; remove foil. Bake 40-50 minutes longer or until crust is lightly browned and filling is bubbly. Cool on a wire rack. Store in the refrigerator. **Yield:** 6-8 servings.

Cranberry-Apple Mincemeat Pies

Lucinda Burton, Scarborough, Ontario

Traditional mincemeat is too heavy for me, but this fruity version hits the spot. Others agree—few folks who've tried it stop at just one slice! I often get recipe requests.

- 4 cups fresh *or* frozen cranberries, thawed
- 4 cups chopped peeled tart apples
- 1-1/2 cups chopped dried apricots
- 1-1/2 cups golden raisins
- 1 medium unpeeled navel orange, finely chopped
- 1/4 cup *each* red and green candied cherries
- 2-3/4 cups sugar
- 1 cup apple juice
- 1/4 cup butter *or* margarine
- 1/4 cup orange marmalade
- 1 teaspoon ground ginger
- 3/4 teaspoon *each* ground allspice, cinnamon and nutmeg
- Pastry for double-crust pie (9 inches)

In a Dutch oven or large kettle, combine the fruit, sugar, apple juice, butter, marmalade and spices. Bring to a boil over medium heat. Reduce heat; simmer, uncovered, for 50-60 minutes, stirring occasionally. Cool completely or refrigerate for up to 1 week. Line two 9-in. pie plates with pastry; trim and flute edges. Divide filling between crusts. Cover edges loosely with foil. Bake at 400° for 20 minutes. Remove foil. Bake 20-25 minutes longer or until crust is golden brown and filling is bubbly. Cool on wire racks. **Yield:** 2 pies (6-8 servings each). **Editor's Note:** Mincemeat mixture may be frozen for up to 3 months. Thaw in the refrigerator.

Berry Cream Pie

Susan Yaeger, Boone, Iowa

(Pictured below and on cover)

I found this recipe in a very old cookbook and made it for a family gathering. The pie was gone in no time. It's a perfect summertime treat.

FILLING:

- 1/2 cup sugar
- 3 tablespoons cornstarch
- 3 tablespoons all-purpose flour
- 1/2 teaspoon salt
- 2 cups milk
- 1 egg, lightly beaten
- 1/2 teaspoon vanilla extract
- 1/2 teaspoon almond extract, optional
- 1/2 cup whipping cream
- 1 pastry shell (9 inches), baked

GLAZE:

- 1/2 cup crushed strawberries
- 1/2 cup water
- 1/4 cup sugar
- 2 teaspoons cornstarch
- 1-1/2 cups quartered strawberries
- 1-1/2 cups fresh raspberries

In a saucepan, combine sugar, cornstarch, flour and salt; gradually stir in milk until smooth. Cook and stir over medium-high heat until thickened and bubbly. Reduce heat; cook and stir 2 minutes more. Remove from the heat and stir a small amount into egg; return all to the saucepan. Cook and stir until almost bubbly. Reduce heat; cook and stir 1-2 minutes more (do not boil). Remove from the heat; stir in vanilla and almond extract if desired. Cool to room temperature. Whip cream; fold into filling. Pour into pastry shell. Chill for at least 2 hours. About 2 hours before serving, prepare glaze. Combine crushed strawberries and water in a saucepan; cook for 2 minutes. Combine sugar and cornstarch; gradually stir into the berries. Cook until thickened and clear, stirring constantly. Strain. Cool for 20 minutes. Meanwhile, arrange quartered strawberries and raspberries over filling; pour glaze evenly over berries. Refrigerate for 1 hour. **Yield:** 6-8 servings.

Cran-Raspberry Pie

Verona Koehlmoos, Pilger, Nebraska

Jewel-toned fruits team up to pack this pretty pie with festive flavor. Our four grown children especially enjoy this dessert when they come home for family holiday meals.

- 2 cups chopped fresh *or* frozen cranberries
- 1 package (12 ounces) unsweetened frozen raspberries
- 1-1/2 cups sugar
- 2 tablespoons quick-cooking tapioca
- 1/2 teaspoon almond extract
- 1/4 teaspoon salt
- Pastry for double-crust pie (9 inches)

In a bowl, gently stir cranberries, raspberries, sugar, tapioca, extract and salt; let stand for 15 minutes. Line a 9-in. pie plate with bottom pastry; add filling. Make a lattice crust. Trim, seal and flute edges. Bake at 375° for 15 minutes. Reduce heat to 350° and bake 35-40 minutes longer or until bubbly. Cool on a wire rack. **Yield:** 6-8 servings.

Peach Plum Pie

Susan Osborne, Hatfield Point, New Brunswick

(Pictured below)

When I want to impress guests, this is the pie I prepare. Peaches, plums and a bit of lemon peel are a refreshing trio that wakes up taste buds. It's a family favorite that's requested often.

- 2 cups sliced peeled fresh *or* frozen peaches, thawed and drained
- 2 cups sliced peeled fresh purple plums
- 1 tablespoon lemon juice
- 1/4 teaspoon almond extract
- 1-1/2 cups sugar
- 1/4 cup quick-cooking tapioca
- 1/2 to 1 teaspoon grated lemon peel
- 1/4 teaspoon salt
- Pastry for double-crust pie (9 inches)
- 2 tablespoons butter *or* margarine

In a large bowl, combine the peaches, plums, lemon juice and extract. In another bowl, combine sugar, tapioca, lemon peel and salt. Add to fruit mixture and stir gently; let stand for 15 minutes. Line a 9-in. pie plate with bottom crust; add the filling. Dot with butter. Roll out remaining pastry to fit top of pie. Place over filling. Trim, seal and flute edges. Cut slits in pastry. Cover the edges loosely with foil. Bake at 450° for 10 minutes. Reduce heat to 350°. Remove foil; bake 35 minutes longer or until crust is golden brown and filling is bubbly. Cool on a wire rack. **Yield:** 6-8 servings.

Rhubarb Raspberry Pie

Lynda Bailey, Sandpoint, Idaho

My family loves rhubarb and raspberries, so I was happy to find this recipe several years ago. The pie always brings smiles to their faces whenever I set it on the dinner table.

- 1 cup sugar
- 1/4 cup quick-cooking tapioca
- 4 cups chopped fresh *or* frozen rhubarb
- 1 cup fresh *or* frozen raspberries
- 2 tablespoons lemon juice
- Pastry for double-crust pie (9 inches)

In a large bowl, combine sugar and tapioca. Add the rhubarb, raspberries and lemon juice; mix gently. Let stand for 15 minutes. Line a 9-in. pie plate with bottom crust; add filling. Make a lattice crust. Trim, seal and flute edges. Bake at 375° for 45-55 minutes or until crust is golden brown and filling is bubbly. Cool on a wire rack. **Yield:** 6-8 servings.

Thicken with Tapioca

Quick-cooking tapioca is the preferred thickener for fruit pies because it doesn't add any flavor and can help preserve the color of fruits. Plus, tapioca absorbs and thickens the fruit juice and prevents the filling from bubbling over.

Peach Blueberry Pie

Sue Thumma, Shepherd, Michigan

(Pictured below)

"Boy…I never thought of putting these two together. What a flavor!" That's what I hear most often after folks try this pie I "invented" one day when I was short of peaches for a full crust. The result was so delicious, I make this more often than plain peach pie.

 1 cup sugar
 1/3 cup all-purpose flour
 1/2 teaspoon ground cinnamon
 1/8 teaspoon ground allspice
 3 cups sliced peeled fresh peaches
 1 cup fresh blueberries
 1 tablespoon butter *or* margarine
Pastry for double-crust pie (9 inches)
Milk
Cinnamon-sugar

In a bowl, combine sugar, flour, cinnamon and allspice. Add the peaches and blueberries; toss gently. Line a 9-in. pie plate with bottom crust; add filling. Dot with butter. Roll out remaining pastry; make a lattice crust. Trim, seal and flute edges. Brush lattice top with milk; sprinkle with cinnamon-sugar. Bake at 400° for 40-45 minutes or until crust is golden brown and filling is bubbly. Cool on a wire rack. **Yield:** 6-8 servings. **Editor's Note:** Frozen fruit may be used if it is thawed and well drained.

Poppy Seed Strawberry Pie

Kris Sackett, Eau Claire, Wisconsin

(Pictured above)

The combination of flavors in this pretty dessert won me over the first time I tasted it. So I've been making it often ever since. It's an easy yet elegant ending to special-occasion suppers or everyday dinners.

1-1/3 cups all-purpose flour
 1 tablespoon poppy seeds
 1/4 teaspoon salt
 1/2 cup shortening
 3 tablespoons cold water
FILLING:
 2 pints strawberries, *divided*
 2 cups whipped topping
 2 tablespoons honey
 1/4 cup slivered almonds, toasted, optional

In a bowl, combine flour, poppy seeds and salt; cut in shortening until crumbly. Gradually add water, tossing with a fork until dough forms a ball. Roll out pastry to fit a 9-in. pie plate. Transfer pastry to plate; flute edges. Line unpricked pastry with a double thickness of heavy-duty foil. Bake at 450° for 8 minutes. Remove foil; bake 5 minutes longer. Cool on a wire rack. Slice 1 pint of strawberries; fold into whipped topping. Spoon into pie shell. Cut remaining berries in half; arrange over top. Drizzle with honey. Sprinkle with almonds if desired. Refrigerate for at least 1 hour. **Yield:** 6-8 servings.

Mini Apple Pie

Edna Hoffman, Hebron, Indiana

(Pictured above)

I like to try new recipes when apples are in season, and this one was a keeper. Golden Delicious apples are our favorites.

- 1/4 cup golden raisins
- 1/3 cup apple juice
- 2 large Golden Delicious apples (about 1 pound), peeled and sliced
- 2 tablespoons sugar
- 2 tablespoons brown sugar
- 1 tablespoon all-purpose flour
- 1/4 teaspoon ground cinnamon
- Pastry for a single-crust pie (9 inches)

In a saucepan over medium heat, cook raisins in apple juice for 5 minutes. Add apples; cook, uncovered, for 8-10 minutes or until apples are tender. Remove from the heat; cool. Combine the sugars, flour and cinnamon; add to apple mixture. On a floured surface, roll out half of the pastry to fit a 20-oz. baking dish. Transfer pastry to dish; trim to edge of dish. Add filling. Roll out the remaining pastry to fit top of pie; place over filling. Trim, seal and flute edges. Cut slits in pastry. Bake at 400° for 35-40 minutes or until crust is golden brown and filling is bubbly. Cool on a wire rack. **Yield:** 2 servings.

Cherry Berry Pie

Wanda Van Voorhis, Plain City, Ohio

Every time I bake this dessert a neighbor shared with me, folks rave about it. I'm always looking for new treats to serve my husband and daughter. This one's definitely one of their favorites.

- 1-1/2 cups sugar
- 1/4 cup plus 2 teaspoons quick-cooking tapioca

- 1/8 teaspoon salt
- 2-1/2 cups fresh *or* frozen pitted tart cherries, thawed
- 1-1/2 cups fresh *or* frozen unsweetened raspberries, thawed
- 1 teaspoon lemon juice
- Pastry for double-crust pie (9 inches)
- 1 tablespoon butter *or* margarine

In a bowl, combine sugar, tapioca and salt. Add the cherries, raspberries and lemon juice; toss gently. Let stand for 15 minutes. Line a 9-in. pie plate with bottom pastry. Trim to 1 in. beyond edge of pie plate. Add filling; dot with butter. Roll out remaining pastry; make a lattice crust. Trim, seal and flute high edges. Cover edges loosely with foil. Bake at 400° for 30 minutes. Remove foil; bake 5-10 minutes longer or until crust is golden brown and filling is bubbly. Cool on a wire rack. **Yield:** 6-8 servings.

Rhubarb Custard Pie

Dolly Piper, Racine, Wisconsin

(Pictured below)

My mother always made this scrumptious pie with the first rhubarb picked. It's one of my earliest memories of a favorite treat, so I feel lucky to have this recipe.

- 1-1/2 cups all-purpose flour
- 1/4 teaspoon salt
- 1/2 cup shortening
- 1/4 cup cold water
- 3 to 4 cups diced fresh *or* frozen rhubarb, thawed and drained
- 1-1/2 cups sugar
- 2 tablespoons cornstarch
- 3/4 teaspoon ground nutmeg
- 2 eggs

In a bowl, combine flour and salt. Cut in shortening until mixture resembles coarse crumbs. Sprinkle with water, 1 tablespoon at a time, and toss lightly with a fork until the dough forms a ball. On a floured surface, roll out dough to fit a 9-in. pie plate. Place rhubarb in pie shell. In a small bowl, combine sugar, cornstarch, nutmeg and eggs; mix well. Pour over rhubarb. Bake at 375° for 45 minutes or until crust is golden brown and filling is bubbly. Cool on a wire rack. Store in the refrigerator. **Yield:** 6-8 servings.

Blueberry Cream Pie

Kim Erickson, Sturgis, Michigan

(Pictured above)

Whenever I ask my family which pie they'd like me to make, everyone gives the same answer—Blueberry Cream Pie!

1-1/3 cups vanilla wafer crumbs
2 tablespoons sugar
5 tablespoons butter *or* margarine, melted
1/2 teaspoon vanilla extract
FILLING:
1/4 cup sugar
3 tablespoons all-purpose flour
Pinch salt
1 cup half-and-half cream
3 egg yolks, beaten
3 tablespoons butter *or* margarine
1 teaspoon vanilla extract
1 tablespoon confectioners' sugar
TOPPING:
5 cups fresh blueberries, *divided*
2/3 cup sugar
1 tablespoon cornstarch

Combine the first four ingredients; press onto the bottom and sides of an ungreased 9-in. pie plate. Bake at 350° for 8-10 minutes or until crust just begins to brown. Cool. In a saucepan, combine sugar, flour and salt.

Gradually whisk in cream; cook and stir over medium heat until thickened and bubbly. Cook and stir 2 minutes more. Gradually whisk half into egg yolks; return all to pan. Bring to a gentle boil; cook and stir 2 minutes. Remove from the heat; stir in butter and vanilla until butter is melted. Cool for 5 minutes, stirring occasionally. Pour into crust; sprinkle with confectioners' sugar. Chill 30 minutes or until set. Meanwhile, crush 2 cups of blueberries in a saucepan; bring to a boil. Boil 2 minutes, stirring constantly. Press berries through sieve; set aside 1 cup juice (add water if necessary). Discard pulp. In a saucepan, combine sugar and cornstarch. Gradually stir in blueberry juice; bring to a boil. Boil 2 minutes, stirring constantly. Remove from the heat; cool 15 minutes. Gently stir in remaining berries; carefully spoon over filling. Chill 3 hours or until set. Store in the refrigerator. **Yield:** 6-8 servings.

Fresh Apricot Pie

Ruth Peterson, Jenison, Michigan

This dessert is a nice change of pace from the more traditional fruit and berry pies. Apricots are very nutritious and delicious!

4 cups sliced fresh apricots
1 cup sugar
1/3 cup all-purpose flour
Pinch ground nutmeg
1 tablespoon lemon juice
Pastry for double-crust pie (9 inches)
Milk
Additional sugar

In a bowl, toss apricots, sugar, flour and nutmeg. Sprinkle with lemon juice; mix well. Line a 9-in. pie plate with bottom crust; add filling. Make a lattice crust. Trim, seal and flute edges. Brush with milk and sprinkle with sugar. Cover edges loosely with foil. Bake at 375° for 45-55 minutes or until golden brown. Cool on a wire rack. **Yield:** 6-8 servings.

Farm Apple Pan Pie

Dolores Skrout, Summerhill, Pennsylvania

(Pictured below)

You'll find this pie's very convenient for taking to a covered-dish supper, picnic, etc. But be prepared—people always ask for a copy of the recipe!

EGG YOLK PASTRY:
    5 cups all-purpose flour
    4 teaspoons sugar
    1/2 teaspoon salt
    1/2 teaspoon baking powder
1-1/2 cups shortening
    2 egg yolks, lightly beaten
    3/4 cup cold water
FILLING:
    5 pounds tart apples, peeled and thinly sliced
    4 teaspoons lemon juice
    3/4 cup sugar
    3/4 cup packed brown sugar
    1 teaspoon ground cinnamon
    1/2 teaspoon ground nutmeg
    1/4 teaspoon salt
Milk
Additional sugar

In a bowl, combine flour, sugar, salt and baking powder; cut in shortening until the mixture resembles coarse crumbs. Combine yolks and water. Sprinkle over dry ingredients; toss with fork. If needed, add additional water, 1 tablespoon at a time, until dough forms a ball. Divide dough in half. On a lightly floured surface, roll half of dough to fit a 15-in. x 10-in. x 1-in. baking pan. Sprinkle apples with lemon juice; arrange half over dough. Combine the sugars, cinnamon, nutmeg and salt; sprinkle half over apples. Top with remaining apples; sprinkle with remaining sugar mixture. Roll remaining pastry to fit pan; place over filling and seal edges. Brush with milk and sprinkle with sugar. Cut slits in top pastry. Bake at 400° for 50 minutes or until crust is golden brown and filling is bubbly. Cool on a wire rack. **Yield:** 18-24 servings.

Fresh Raspberry Pie

Patricia Staudt, Marble Rock, Iowa

(Pictured above)

Mouth-watering fresh raspberries star in this luscious pie. There's nothing to distract from the tangy berry flavor and gorgeous ruby color. A big slice is an excellent way to enjoy the taste of summer.

    1/4 cup sugar
    1 tablespoon cornstarch
    1 cup water
    1 package (3 ounces) raspberry gelatin
    4 cups fresh raspberries
    1 graham cracker crust (9 inches)

In a saucepan, combine sugar and cornstarch. Stir in water until smooth; bring to a boil, stirring constantly. Cook and stir for 2 minutes. Remove from the heat; stir in gelatin until dissolved. Cool for 15 minutes. Place raspberries in the crust; slowly pour gelatin mixture over berries. Chill until set, about 3 hours. **Yield:** 6-8 servings.

Banana Blueberry Pie

Priscilla Weaver, Hagerstown, Maryland

This light fruity dessert is so simple to prepare. It makes two, so you have one pie for guests and a second to enjoy the next day.

    1 package (8 ounces) cream cheese, softened
    3/4 cup sugar
    2 cups whipped topping
    4 medium firm bananas, sliced
    2 pastry shells (9 inches), baked
    1 can (21 ounces) blueberry pie filling
Fresh blueberries and mint and additional sliced bananas, optional

In a mixing bowl, beat cream cheese and sugar until smooth. Fold in whipped topping and bananas. Pour into pastry shells. Spread with pie filling. Refrigerate for at least 30 minutes. Just before serving, garnish with blueberries, mint and bananas if desired. **Yield:** 2 pies (6-8 servings each).

Macaroon Cherry Pie

Lori Daniels, Beverly, West Virginia

I use homegrown cherries in this bountiful pie with its unique crunchy coconut topping. But I've found that purchased tart cherries yield a dessert that's nearly as delicious. I always bake this pie around Presidents' Day or Valentine's Day, but it's popular with my family in any season.

Pastry for single-crust pie (9 inches)
   3 cans (14-1/2 ounces *each*) pitted tart cherries
   1 cup sugar
   1/3 cup cornstarch
   1/2 teaspoon ground cinnamon
   1/4 teaspoon red food coloring, optional
TOPPING:
   1 egg, lightly beaten
   2 tablespoons milk
   1 tablespoon butter *or* margarine, melted
   1/4 teaspoon almond extract
   1/4 cup sugar
   1/8 teaspoon salt
   1 cup flaked coconut
   1/2 cup sliced almonds

Line a 9-in. deep-dish pie plate with pastry. Trim to 1/2 in. beyond edge of plate; flute edges. Bake at 400° for 6 minutes; set aside. Drain cherries, reserving 1 cup juice. Set cherries aside. In a saucepan, combine sugar and cornstarch; gradually stir in cherry juice until smooth. Bring to a boil over medium heat; cook and stir for 2 minutes or until thickened. Remove from the heat; stir in cinnamon and food coloring if desired. Gently fold in cherries. Pour into crust. Cover edges loosely with foil. Bake at 400° for 20 minutes. Meanwhile, in a bowl, combine the first six topping ingredients. Stir in coconut and almonds. Remove foil from pie; spoon topping over pie. Return to the oven; reduce heat to 350°. Bake for 20 minutes or until topping is lightly browned. Cool on a wire rack for 1 hour. Chill for at least 4 hours or overnight before cutting. **Yield:** 6-8 servings.

Creamy Pear Pie

Kathryn Gross, Fontanelle, Iowa

(Pictured above right)

There aren't many recipes using fresh pears. I heard this recipe on the radio while I was driving the tractor in the field. I kept repeating the ingredients over and over until it was time to go in the house for lunch, then I wrote the recipe down on paper. We enjoy it every summer.

   4 cups sliced peeled pears
   1/3 cup sugar
   2 tablespoons all-purpose flour
   1 cup (8 ounces) sour cream
   1/2 teaspoon vanilla extract
   1/2 teaspoon lemon extract
   1/2 teaspoon almond extract
   1 unbaked pastry shell (9 inches)
TOPPING:
   1/4 cup all-purpose flour
   2 tablespoons butter *or* margarine, melted
   2 tablespoons brown sugar

In a large bowl, toss the pears with sugar and flour. Combine the sour cream and vanilla, lemon and almond extracts; add to pear mixture and mix well. Pour into pastry shell. For topping, in a small bowl, mix the flour, butter and brown sugar until crumbly. Sprinkle over the pears. Bake at 400° for 10 minutes. Reduce heat to 350°; bake 45 minutes longer or until the pears are tender. Cool on a wire rack. Store in the refrigerator. **Yield:** 6-8 servings.

Preventing Soggy Crusts

Wait to pour a pie filling into a pastry shell until just before baking. Combining the two ahead of time and letting the unbaked pie stand contributes to a soggy bottom crust.

German Apple Pie

Mrs. Woodrow Taylor, Adams Center, New York

I live in a big apple-producing state, so I think this recipe represents our region well. I first tasted this apple pie many years ago when my children's baby-sitter made it. I asked for the recipe and have made it many times myself since.

        1-1/2 cups all-purpose flour
         1/2 teaspoon salt
         1/2 cup shortening
           1 teaspoon vanilla extract
           2 to 3 tablespoons cold water
    FILLING:
           1 cup sugar
         1/4 cup all-purpose flour
           2 teaspoons ground cinnamon
           6 cups sliced peeled tart apples
           1 cup whipping cream
    Whipped cream, optional

In a bowl, combine flour and salt; cut in shortening until the mixture resembles coarse crumbs. Sprinkle with vanilla. Gradually add water, tossing with a fork until dough forms a ball. On a lightly floured surface, roll the pastry to fit a 9-in. pie plate; trim and flute edges. For filling, combine sugar, flour and cinnamon; sprinkle 3 tablespoons into crust. Top with half of the apples. Sprinkle with half of the remaining sugar mixture. Top with remaining apples and sugar mixture. Pour whipping cream over all. Bake at 450° for 10 minutes. Reduce heat to 350°; bake 55-60 minutes longer or until the apples are tender. Cool on a wire rack. Store in the refrigerator. Serve with whipped cream if desired. **Yield:** 6-8 servings.

Glazed Blackberry Pie

Monica Gross, Downey, California

(Pictured above)

This scrumptious pie is easy to assemble. But the impressive results will have people thinking you spent hours in the kitchen.

           5 cups fresh blackberries, *divided*
           1 pastry shell (9 inches), baked
           1 cup water, *divided*
         3/4 cup sugar
           3 tablespoons cornstarch
    Red food coloring, optional
    Whipped topping

Place 2 cups blackberries in pastry shell; set aside. In a saucepan, crush 1 cup berries. Add 3/4 cup water. Bring to a boil over medium heat, stirring constantly. Cook and stir for 2 minutes. Press berries through a sieve. Set juice aside and discard pulp. In a saucepan, combine the sugar and cornstarch. Stir in remaining water and reserved juice until smooth. Bring to a boil; cook and stir for 2 minutes or until thickened. Remove from the heat; stir in food coloring if desired. Pour half of the glaze over berries in pastry shell. Stir remaining berries into remaining glaze; carefully spoon over filling. Refrigerate for 3 hours or until set. Garnish with whipped topping. Store in the refrigerator. **Yield:** 6-8 servings.

Spring and Fall Pie

Laura Collins, Rapid City, South Dakota

Fresh Fruit Pies

Every spring, I have fresh rhubarb, and one of my favorite ways to use it is in this pie. I adapted this from a recipe I received from our county Extension service.

1-1/2 cups sugar
   3 tablespoons all-purpose flour
1-1/2 cups diced fresh *or* frozen rhubarb, thawed and drained
1-1/2 cups fresh *or* frozen cranberries, halved
1-1/2 cups chopped peeled tart apples
Pastry for double-crust pie (9 inches)

In a large bowl, combine sugar and flour; stir in rhubarb, cranberries and apples. Line a 9-in. pie plate with the bottom pastry; add filling. Make a lattice crust; trim, seal and flute edges. Bake at 450° for 10 minutes. Reduce heat to 350°; bake 40 minutes longer or until crust is golden brown and filling is bubbly. Cover edges with foil to prevent overbrowning if necessary. Cool on a wire rack. **Yield:** 6-8 servings.

Perfect Rhubarb Pie

Ellen Benninger, Stoneboro, Pennsylvania

(Pictured below)

Nothing hides the tangy rhubarb in this lovely pie, which has just the right balance of sweet and tart. It's a wonderful way to celebrate the end of winter!

   4 cups sliced fresh *or* frozen rhubarb
   4 cups boiling water
1-1/2 cups sugar
   3 tablespoons all-purpose flour
   1 teaspoon quick-cooking tapioca
   1 egg
   2 teaspoons cold water
Pastry for double-crust pie (9 inches)
   1 tablespoon butter *or* margarine

Place rhubarb in a colander and pour boiling water over it; set aside. In a bowl, combine sugar, flour and tapioca; mix well. Add drained rhubarb; toss to coat. Let stand for 15 minutes. Beat egg and cold water; add to rhubarb mixture and mix well. Line a 9-in. pie plate with bottom pastry. Add filling. Dot with butter. Cover with remaining pastry; flute edges. Cut slits in top crust. Bake at 400° for 15 minutes. Reduce heat to 350°; bake 40-50 minutes longer or until crust is golden brown and filling is bubbly. Cool on a wire rack. Store in the refrigerator. **Yield:** 6-8 servings.

Easy Cranberry Pie

Marjorie Carey, Belfry, Montana

(Pictured above)

As a special treat when making this pie, Mom would sometimes place a marshmallow in the center of each lattice square, or, in honor of the Christmas tree we had just brought home, she'd cut Christmas tree shapes from the pie dough and place them on top of the pie.

   2 cans (16 ounces *each*) whole-berry cranberry sauce
1/4 cup packed brown sugar
   2 tablespoons butter *or* margarine, softened
Pastry for double-crust pie (9 inches)

In a bowl, combine cranberry sauce, brown sugar and butter. Line a 9-in. pie plate with bottom pastry; add filling. Make a lattice crust. Trim, seal and flute edges. Bake at 350° for 50-60 minutes or until the crust is lightly browned. **Yield:** 6-8 servings. **Editor's Note:** For a festively decorated pie, use a cookie cutter to cut out Christmas tree shapes from the top pastry instead of using a lattice crust. Place the dough shapes on an ungreased baking sheet and bake at 350° for 10-15 minutes or until golden. Cool slightly; arrange over filling of baked pie.

1-1/4 cups sugar, *divided*
1/4 cup all-purpose flour
1/4 teaspoon salt
3 tablespoons orange juice concentrate
1/4 cup butter *or* margarine, melted
3 eggs, *separated*
2-1/2 cups diced rhubarb (1/2-inch pieces)
1 unbaked pastry shell (9 inches)
1/3 cup chopped walnuts

In a large bowl, combine 1 cup sugar, flour and salt. Stir in orange juice and butter. In a small bowl, lightly beat egg yolks; stir into the orange juice mixture. Add rhubarb. In a mixing bowl, beat egg whites until soft peaks begin to form; gradually beat in remaining sugar until stiff peaks form. Fold into rhubarb mixture. Pour into pie shell. Sprinkle with nuts. Bake at 375° for 15 minutes. Reduce heat to 325°; bake for 40 minutes or until golden. If needed, cover pie loosely with foil during the last 10 minutes to prevent excess browning. Cool on a wire rack for 1 hour. Store in the refrigerator. **Yield:** 6-8 servings.

Raspberry Meringue Pie

Mrs. Anton Sohrwiede, McGraw, New York

(Pictured above)

We have raspberry bushes, so I'm always looking for recipes using this delicious fruit. This is one of my most requested recipes.

1 cup all-purpose flour
1/3 cup sugar
1 teaspoon baking powder
1/4 teaspoon salt
2 tablespoons cold butter *or* margarine
1 egg, beaten
2 tablespoons milk
TOPPING:
2 egg whites
1/2 cup sugar
2 cups unsweetened raspberries

In a bowl, combine the flour, sugar, baking powder and salt; cut in butter. Combine egg and milk; stir into flour mixture (dough will be sticky). Press onto the bottom and up the sides of a greased 9-in. pie plate; set aside. In a mixing bowl, beat egg whites on medium speed until soft peaks form. Gradually beat in sugar, 1 tablespoon at a time, until stiff peaks form. Fold into raspberries. Spoon over the crust. Bake at 350° for 30-35 minutes or until browned. Cool on a wire rack for 1 hour. Store in the refrigerator. **Yield:** 6-8 servings.

Orange Rhubarb Pie

Mrs. M.E. Kaufman, Haines City, Florida

This is one of my favorite ways to use our rhubarb crop. The combination of rhubarb and orange gives this pie a nice flavor.

Triple Fruit Pie

Jeanne Freybler, Grand Rapids, Michigan

(Pictured below)

My goal is to create pies as good as my mother's. The first time I made this one, my family begged for seconds. If I continue making pies this good, maybe someday our two daughters will be striving to imitate mine!

1-1/4 cups *each* fresh blueberries, raspberries and chopped rhubarb*

1/2 teaspoon almond extract
1-1/4 cups sugar
1/4 cup quick-cooking tapioca
1/4 teaspoon ground nutmeg
1/4 teaspoon salt
1 tablespoon lemon juice
Pastry for double-crust pie (9 inches)

In a large bowl, combine fruits and extract; toss to coat. In another bowl, combine sugar, tapioca, nutmeg and salt. Add to fruit; stir gently. Let stand for 15 minutes. Line a 9-in. pie plate with bottom crust; trim pastry even with edge. Stir lemon juice into fruit mixture; spoon into the crust. Roll out remaining pastry; make a lattice crust. Trim, seal and flute edges. Bake at 400° for 20 minutes. Reduce heat to 350°; bake 30 minutes longer or until the crust is golden brown and the filling is bubbly. Cool on a wire rack. **Yield:** 6-8 servings. ***Editor's Note:** Frozen blueberries, raspberries and rhubarb may be substituted for fresh; thaw and drain before using.

Fruit 'n' Nut Cherry Pie

Ruth Andrewson, Leavenworth, Washington

It's a pleasure to serve this festive ruby-colored pie, which tastes as good as it looks! The filling is an irresistible combination of fruits and nuts. Topped with a bit of whipped cream, a lovely slice of this pie is a cool refreshing end to an enjoyable meal.

3/4 cup sugar
1 tablespoon cornstarch
1 can (21 ounces) cherry pie filling
1 can (20 ounces) crushed pineapple, undrained
1 teaspoon red food coloring, optional
4 medium firm bananas, sliced
1/2 cup chopped pecans *or* walnuts
2 pastry shells (9 inches), baked
Whipped cream

In a saucepan, combine sugar, cornstarch, cherry pie filling, pineapple and food coloring if desired; mix well. Bring to a boil over medium heat, stirring constantly. Cook and stir for 2 minutes. Cool. Fold in bananas and nuts. Pour into pastry shells. Chill for 2-3 hours. Garnish with whipped cream. Store in the refrigerator. **Yield:** 12-16 servings.

Which Pies to Refrigerate

Refrigerate pies containing dairy products or eggs. Pies made with eggs, milk, sour cream, whipped cream, whipped topping, yogurt or cream cheese should be refrigerated as soon as possible after they've been prepared or about 1 hour after baking.

Glazed Pineapple Pie

Kathy Crow, Cordova, Alaska

(Pictured above)

With its unique glaze, this pie is a tropical treat. It makes a pretty presentation on your table any time of year.

1 cup sugar
1/4 cup all-purpose flour
1 can (20 ounces) crushed pineapple
1 tablespoon lemon juice
1 tablespoon butter *or* margarine, melted
1/4 teaspoon salt
Pastry for double-crust pie (9 inches)
3/4 cup flaked coconut
1/2 cup confectioners' sugar
1/4 teaspoon vanilla extract

Drain pineapple, reserving 1 tablespoon juice for glaze. In a bowl, combine sugar, flour, pineapple, lemon juice, butter and salt; mix well and set aside. Line a 9-in. pie plate with the bottom pastry. Sprinkle with coconut. Spread pineapple mixture over coconut. Top with remaining pastry; flute edges and cut slits in top. Bake at 400° for 35-40 minutes or until golden brown. Cool on a wire rack for 20 minutes. Meanwhile, for glaze, combine confectioners' sugar, vanilla and reserved pineapple juice until smooth. Spread over the top of warm pie. **Yield:** 6-8 servings. **Editor's Note:** To decorate top of pie with cutouts as shown in photo, use a small pineapple-shaped cookie cutter to cut shapes from top pastry before placing pastry over filling. Place dough shapes on an ungreased baking sheet and bake at 350° for 8-10 minutes or until golden. Cool slightly; arrange over baked pie after glazing.

Strawberry Meringue Pie

Kathleen Mercier, Orrington, Maine

(Pictured above)

This great dessert is simple, so don't be put off by the long directions. It's impressive-looking to serve to guests.

  1/3 cup finely crushed saltines (about 12
      crackers), *divided*
    3 egg whites
  1/4 teaspoon cream of tartar
  1/8 teaspoon salt
    1 cup sugar
    1 teaspoon vanilla extract
  1/2 cup chopped pecans, toasted
    1 package (4 ounces) German sweet
      chocolate
    2 tablespoons butter (no substitutes)
    4 cups strawberries, halved
    1 cup whipping cream
    2 tablespoons confectioners' sugar

Sprinkle 2 tablespoons cracker crumbs into a greased 9-in. pie plate. In a mixing bowl, beat egg whites, cream of tartar and salt until soft peaks form. Gradually add sugar; beat until stiff peaks form. Fold in the vanilla, pecans and remaining cracker crumbs. Spread meringue onto the bottom and up the sides of prepared pan. Bake at 350° for 25-30 minutes or until meringue is lightly browned. Cool on a wire rack. Melt chocolate and butter; drizzle over shell. Let stand 15 minutes or until set. Top with berries. Whip the cream and confectioners' sugar until soft peaks form; spoon over berries. **Yield:** 6-8 servings.

Cream Cheese Rhubarb Pie

Beverly Kuhn, Orwell, Ohio

Whenever my mom and I have a "rhubarb attack", we make this pie! It's a scrumptious way to put that tangy produce to good use. The cream cheese topping is a tasty addition.

  1/4 cup cornstarch
    1 cup sugar
Pinch salt
  1/2 cup water
    3 cups sliced fresh *or* frozen rhubarb
      (1/2-inch pieces)
    1 unbaked pastry shell (9 inches)
TOPPING:
    1 package (8 ounces) cream cheese,
      softened
    2 eggs
  1/2 cup sugar
Whipped cream
Sliced almonds

In a saucepan, combine the cornstarch, sugar and salt. Add water; stir until smooth. Add the sliced rhubarb. Bring to a boil. Cook and stir for 2 minutes or until thickened and bubbly. Pour into the pastry shell; bake at 425° for 10 minutes. Meanwhile, for topping, in a mixing bowl, beat cream cheese, eggs and sugar until smooth. Pour over the top of the pie. Return to the oven; reduce heat to 325°. Bake for 35 minutes or until set. Cool for 1 hour on a wire rack. Refrigerate several hours or overnight. Garnish with whipped cream and sliced almonds. **Yield:** 8 servings.

Plum Pie

Shirley Smith, Noti, Oregon

(Pictured below)

My husband says this pie's his favorite. But he claims to only like two kinds of pies—warm and cold ones.

Pastry for double-crust pie (9 inches)
   1/4 cup packed brown sugar
   1/4 cup saltine crumbs
1-1/2 pounds fresh plums, pitted and quartered
    1 cup sugar
   1/4 cup all-purpose flour
    1 teaspoon ground cinnamon
    3 tablespoons cold butter *or* **margarine**
    1 teaspoon cinnamon-sugar

Line a 9-in. pie plate with bottom crust. Combine brown sugar and crumbs. Sprinkle over pastry and press gently. Cover with plums. Combine the sugar, flour and cinnamon; cut in butter until crumbly. Sprinkle over plums. Roll out remaining pastry to fit top of pie; place over plums. Seal and flute edges; cut slits in top. Sprinkle with cinnamon-sugar. Bake at 400° for 30 minutes. Reduce heat to 350°; bake 25 minutes longer or until golden brown. Cool on a wire rack. **Yield:** 6-8 servings.

Peach Cream Pie

Denise Goedeken, Platte Center, Nebraska

This yummy pie is a sure winner when fresh peaches are in season. The sour cream filling and cinnamon crumb topping complement the fruit flavor.

1-1/2 cups all-purpose flour
   1/2 teaspoon salt
   1/2 cup cold butter *or* **margarine**
FILLING:
    4 cups unsweetened sliced peaches
    1 cup sugar, *divided*
    2 tablespoons all-purpose flour
    1 egg
   1/2 teaspoon vanilla extract
   1/4 teaspoon salt

    1 cup (8 ounces) sour cream
TOPPING:
   1/3 cup sugar
   1/3 cup all-purpose flour
    1 teaspoon ground cinnamon
   1/4 cup cold butter *or* **margarine**

Combine flour and salt; cut in butter until crumbly. Press into a 9-in. pie plate. Sprinkle peaches with 1/4 cup sugar. Combine flour, egg, vanilla, salt and remaining sugar; fold in sour cream. Stir into peaches; pour into crust. Bake at 400° for 15 minutes. Reduce heat to 350°; bake for 20 minutes. For topping, combine sugar, flour and cinnamon in a small bowl; cut in butter until crumbly. Sprinkle over the pie. Return oven temperature to 400°; bake 15 minutes longer. Cool on a wire rack for 1 hour. Store in the refrigerator. **Yield:** 6-8 servings.

Horn of Plenty Pie

Liz Fernald, Mashpee, Massachusetts

(Pictured above)

I especially like making this pie during the holidays. Since we live on Cape Cod, we have access to abandoned cranberry bogs.

1-1/2 cups sugar
   1/3 cup water
    3 cups fresh *or* **frozen cranberries**
   1/2 cup raisins
   1/2 cup chopped walnuts
   1/2 cup chopped peeled tart apple
    1 tablespoon butter *or* **margarine**
Pinch salt
    1 unpricked pastry shell (9 inches), baked
MERINGUE:
    3 egg whites
    6 tablespoons brown sugar

In a large saucepan, bring sugar and water to a boil. Add cranberries, raisins, walnuts and apple; cover and simmer for 15 minutes, stirring occasionally. Stir in butter and salt. Spoon into pie shell. In a mixing bowl, beat egg whites until stiff peaks form; gradually beat in sugar. Pour over hot filling, sealing to edges of pastry. Bake at 350° for 15 minutes or until golden brown. Cool on a wire rack for 1 hour. Store in the refrigerator. **Yield:** 6-8 servings.

p. 56

p. 41

p. 59

p. 54

p. 46

Custard, Pudding & Cream Pies

CREAM OF THE CROP. Clockwise from upper left: Fudgy Pecan Pie (p. 41), Cream Puff Pie (p. 56), Lemon Supreme Pie (p. 59), Chocolate Banana Cream Pie (p. 46) and Maple Pecan Pie (p. 54).

Raisin Butterscotch Pie

Arleen Owen, Fresno, California

I won a county fair ribbon for this quick dessert. Many of the recipes I've entered through the years have included our state's famous raisins.

>   2 cups cold milk
>   1 package (3.4 ounces) instant vanilla pudding mix
>   1 package (3.4 ounces) instant butterscotch pudding mix
>   2 cups (16 ounces) sour cream
>   1 cup raisins
>   1 medium firm banana, sliced
>   1 pastry shell (9 inches), baked
> Frozen whipped topping, thawed

In a mixing bowl, combine milk and pudding mixes; beat on low speed for 2 minutes. Fold in sour cream; stir in raisins. Place banana slices in pastry shell; top with pudding mixture. Chill until serving. Garnish with whipped topping. **Yield:** 6-8 servings.

Creamy Apricot Pie

Charlotte Cramer, Othello, Washington

(Pictured below)

I keep this excellent dessert recipe close at hand. It's easy to prepare and so cool and satisfying on a summer day. My husband and sons especially like it.

>   1 can (14 ounces) apricot halves
>   1 egg yolk
>   1 can (12 ounces) evaporated milk
>   1 package (3 ounces) cook-and-serve vanilla pudding mix
>   1 pastry shell (9 inches), baked
>   2 teaspoons cornstarch
>   1 can (5-1/4 ounces) apricot nectar
> 1/4 cup sliced almonds, toasted

Drain apricots, reserving 1/2 cup juice; set apricots aside. In a saucepan, combine egg yolk, milk and reserved apri-

Mom's Lemon Custard Pie

Jeannie Fritson, Kearney, Nebraska

(Pictured above)

My mother often made this pie back when we were growing up over 70 years ago. You might say it's stood the test of time, because today it's still my brother's favorite! The beaten egg whites give it a delicate texture and make this custard pie quite unique. It's a great way to top off any meal.

>   1 tablespoon butter *or* margarine, softened
>   1 cup sugar
>   3 tablespoons all-purpose flour
> 1/8 teaspoon salt
>   2 eggs, *separated*
>   1 cup milk
> 1/4 cup lemon juice
> Peel of 1 medium lemon
>   1 unbaked pastry shell (9 inches)
> Whipped cream, optional

Using a spoon, cream butter and sugar in a bowl until well mixed. Add flour, salt, egg yolks and milk; mix well. Add lemon juice and peel; mix well. Set aside. In a small bowl, beat egg whites until stiff peaks form; gently fold into lemon mixture. Pour into pastry shell. Bake at 325° for 1 hour or until lightly browned and a knife inserted near the center comes out clean. Cool on a wire rack for 1 hour. Store in the refrigerator. Garnish with whipped cream if desired. **Yield:** 6-8 servings.

cot juice; stir in the pudding mix until smooth. Bring to a boil over medium heat; cook and stir until thickened. Chop 1/2 cup apricots; add to pudding. Pour into pastry shell. Refrigerate. For glaze, combine cornstarch and apricot nectar in a saucepan until smooth. Bring to a boil over medium heat; cook and stir for 2 minutes or until thickened. Cut the remaining apricots into thirds; arrange over pudding layer. Spoon glaze over top. Sprinkle with almonds. Chill until serving. **Yield:** 6-8 servings.

Squash Pie

Joyce Jackson, Bridgetown, Nova Scotia

I adapted this dessert from a pumpkin pie recipe used in my home economics class. Using squash instead of pumpkin makes every bite even more delicious.

1-1/4 cups mashed cooked winter squash
3/4 cup packed brown sugar
2 tablespoons molasses
1-1/4 teaspoons ground cinnamon
3/4 teaspoon salt
3/4 teaspoon ground nutmeg
3/4 teaspoon ground ginger
3 eggs, beaten
1 can (12 ounces) evaporated milk
1 unbaked pastry shell (9 inches)
Whipped cream, optional

In a bowl, combine the first eight ingredients with a wire whisk. Stir in milk. Pour into pastry shell. Bake at 450° for 10 minutes. Reduce heat to 350°; bake for 50-55 minutes or until a knife inserted near the center

comes out clean. Cool on a wire rack for 1 hour. Store in the refrigerator. Serve with whipped cream if desired. **Yield:** 6-8 servings.

Pumpkin Chiffon Pie

Karen Grimes, Stephens City, Virginia

(Pictured above)

Tie up your time? Not this extra-speedy pumpkin pie! It's always a great standby in my kitchen.

1 package (3 ounces) cream cheese, softened
1 tablespoon sugar
1-1/2 cups whipped topping
1 graham cracker crust (9 inches)
1 cup cold milk
2 packages (3.4 ounces *each*) instant vanilla pudding mix
1 can (15 ounces) solid-pack pumpkin
1 teaspoon ground cinnamon
1/2 teaspoon ground ginger
1/4 teaspoon ground cloves
Additional whipped topping and chopped nuts, optional

In a mixing bowl, beat cream cheese and sugar until smooth. Add whipped topping and mix well. Spread into crust. In another bowl, beat milk and pudding mixes on low speed for 2 minutes. Let stand for 3 minutes. Stir in pumpkin and spices; mix well. Spread over cream cheese layer. Chill until serving. Garnish with whipped topping and nuts if desired. **Yield:** 6-8 servings.

Sprinkle with grated lemon peel. Serve immediately. Refrigerate leftovers. **Yield:** 8 servings. **Editor's Note:** The filling is very light in color. It is not topped with additional whipped cream.

Chocolate Peanut Butter Pie

Carole Taylor, Mason City, Iowa

This extra-speedy pie is a great standby for unexpected company. The crust is purchased or prepared ahead, so simply stir the ingredients together and serve.

   1-3/4 cups cold milk
     1 package (3.9 ounces) instant chocolate pudding mix
     1 chocolate crumb crust (8 *or* 9 inches)
     2 cups whipped topping
     4 peanut butter cups (.6 ounce *each*), coarsely chopped

In a mixing bowl, beat milk and pudding mix on low speed for 2 minutes. Pour into crust. Chill for 20 minutes or until filling is thickened. Spread whipped topping over the pudding. Sprinkle with chopped peanut butter cups. Store in the refrigerator. **Yield:** 6-8 servings.

Coffee Cream Pie

Letha DeMoss, Ames, Iowa

I created this sweet coffee-flavored recipe as an entry for our state fair, adding the toffee topping to dress it up. I'm glad I did—the pie won first place and is now a family holiday favorite!

   2/3 cup sugar
   1/2 cup all-purpose flour
   1/2 teaspoon salt
     2 cups milk
     3 tablespoons instant coffee granules, crushed
     3 egg yolks, lightly beaten
     2 tablespoons butter *or* margarine
     2 teaspoons vanilla extract
     1 chocolate crumb crust (8 *or* 9 inches)
TOPPING:
     1 teaspoon instant coffee granules
     1 cup whipping cream
     2 tablespoons confectioners' sugar
   1/2 teaspoon vanilla extract
     1 Heath candy bar (1.4 ounces), crushed

In a saucepan, combine the sugar, flour and salt; gradually stir in milk until smooth. Bring to a boil. Cook and stir for 2 minutes or until thickened. Stir in coffee granules. Gradually stir a small amount into egg yolks; return all to pan. Bring to a gentle boil. Cook and stir 2 minutes more. Remove from the heat; add butter and vanilla. Cool for 30 minutes. Pour into crust; chill. In a mixing bowl, dissolve coffee granules in a small amount of cream. Add sugar, vanilla and remaining cream. Whip

Creamy Banana Pie

Rita Pribyl, Indianapolis, Indiana
(Pictured above)

When friends ask me to share a recipe using bananas, I know instantly this is the best dessert to pass along. Everyone who tastes a slice enjoys its delicious old-fashioned flavor.

     1 envelope unflavored gelatin
   1/4 cup cold water
   3/4 cup sugar
   1/4 cup cornstarch
   1/2 teaspoon salt
  2-3/4 cups milk
     4 egg yolks, beaten
     2 tablespoons butter *or* margarine
     1 tablespoon vanilla extract
     4 medium firm bananas
     1 cup whipping cream, whipped
     1 pastry shell (10 inches), baked
Juice and grated peel of 1 lemon
   1/2 cup apple jelly

Soften gelatin in cold water; set aside. In a saucepan, combine sugar, cornstarch and salt. Stir in the milk until smooth. Cook and stir over medium-high heat until thickened and bubbly. Reduce heat; cook and stir 2 minutes more. Remove from the heat. Stir a small amount of hot filling into yolks. Return all to pan. Bring to a gentle boil. Cook and stir 2 minutes more. Remove from the heat; stir in softened gelatin until dissolved. Stir in butter and vanilla. Cover the custard surface with plastic wrap and chill until no longer warm, about 1 hour. Fold whipped cream into custard. Slice 3 bananas; fold into custard. Spoon into pastry shell. Chill until set, about 4 hours. Just before serving, place lemon juice in a small bowl and slice the remaining banana into it. Melt jelly in a saucepan over low heat. Drain banana; pat dry and arrange over filling. Brush banana with the jelly.

until stiff peaks form. Spread over filling; sprinkle with crushed candy bar. Chill until serving. **Yield:** 6-8 servings.

Fudgy Pecan Pie

Ellen Arndt, Cologne, Minnesota

(Pictured above and on p. 36)

This started out as just a plain chocolate pie that I "dressed up" for company. Now when I serve it, guests often tell me, "Your pie looks too good to eat—but I won't let that stop me!"

- 1 unbaked pastry shell (9 inches)
- 1 package (4 ounces) German sweet chocolate
- 1/4 cup butter (no substitutes)
- 1 can (14 ounces) sweetened condensed milk
- 1/2 cup water
- 2 eggs, beaten
- 1 teaspoon vanilla extract
- 1/4 teaspoon salt
- 1/2 cup chopped pecans

FILLING:
- 1 cup cold milk
- 1 package (3.9 ounces) instant chocolate pudding mix
- 1 cup whipped topping

TOPPING:
- 1 cup whipping cream
- 1 tablespoon confectioners' sugar
- 1 teaspoon vanilla extract

Pecan halves and grated chocolate

Line unpricked pastry shell with a double thickness of heavy-duty foil. Bake at 450° for 5 minutes. Remove foil and set shell aside. Reduce heat to 375°. In a heavy saucepan, melt chocolate and butter. Remove from the heat; stir in milk and water. Add a small amount of hot chocolate mixture to eggs; return all to the pan. Stir in vanilla and salt. Pour into shell; sprinkle with nuts. Cover edges with foil. Bake for 35 minutes or until a knife inserted near the center comes out clean. Remove to a wire rack to cool completely. In a mixing bowl, beat milk and pudding mix on low speed for 2 minutes. Fold in whipped topping. Spread over nut layer; cover and refrigerate. In a mixing bowl, beat cream until soft peaks form. Add sugar and vanilla, beating until stiff peaks form. Spread over pudding layer. Refrigerate until set, about 4 hours. Garnish with pecan halves and grated chocolate. **Yield:** 6-8 servings.

Creamy Lemonade Pie

Carolyn Griffin, Macon, Georgia

(Pictured below)

This luscious lemon pie looks quite elegant for an Easter dinner, yet it requires little effort. Guests will never suspect they're eating a quick-and-easy dessert.

- 1 can (5 ounces) evaporated milk, chilled
- 1 package (3.4 ounces) instant lemon pudding mix
- 2 packages (8 ounces *each*) cream cheese, softened
- 3/4 cup lemonade concentrate
- 1 graham cracker crust (9 inches)

Lemon slices, fresh raspberries and mint leaves, optional

In a mixing bowl, combine milk and pudding mix; beat on low speed for 2 minutes (mixture will be thick). In another mixing bowl, beat cream cheese until light and fluffy, about 3 minutes. Gradually beat in lemonade concentrate. Gradually beat in pudding mixture. Pour into crust. Cover and refrigerate for at least 4 hours. Garnish if desired. **Yield:** 6-8 servings.

Coconut Cream Meringue Pie

Joyce Reece, Mena, Arkansas

(Pictured below)

Every fifth Sunday at our country church, we have a hymn sing and potluck dinner. I always bring this pie, and it goes fast. It's definitely a favorite.

    1 unbaked pastry shell (9 inches)
    6 tablespoons sugar
    5 tablespoons all-purpose flour
    1/4 teaspoon salt
    2 cups milk
    3 egg yolks, lightly beaten
    2 teaspoons vanilla extract
    1 cup flaked coconut
MERINGUE:
    3 egg whites
    1/4 teaspoon cream of tartar
    6 tablespoons sugar
    1/2 cup flaked coconut

Line unpricked pastry shell with a double thickness of heavy-duty foil. Bake at 450° for 8 minutes. Remove foil; bake 5 minutes longer. Cool on a wire rack. Meanwhile, in a saucepan, combine the sugar, flour and salt. Gradually add milk. Cook and stir over medium-high heat until thickened and bubbly. Reduce heat; cook and stir for 2 minutes. Remove from the heat. Stir a small amount of hot milk mixture into egg yolks; return all to the pan, stirring constantly. Bring to a gentle boil; cook and stir for 2 minutes. Remove from the heat; stir in vanilla and coconut. Pour into the pastry shell. For meringue, in a small mixing bowl, beat egg whites and cream of tartar on medium speed until soft peaks

form. Gradually beat in sugar, 1 tablespoon at a time, on high until stiff peaks form. Spread over hot filling, sealing edges to crust. Sprinkle with coconut. Bake at 350° for 15 minutes or until golden brown. Cool on a wire rack for 1 hour. Chill for 1-2 hours before serving. Store in the refrigerator. **Yield:** 6-8 servings.

Cinnamon Chocolate Angel Pie

Donna Torres, Grand Rapids, Minnesota

Our Christmas dinner wouldn't be complete without a festive finale. I've served this satisfying pie for so many years that it's become a holiday tradition.

    2 egg whites
    1/2 teaspoon white vinegar
    1/2 cup sugar
    1/8 to 1/4 teaspoon ground cinnamon
    1 pastry shell (9 inches), baked
FILLING:
    2 egg yolks
    1/4 cup water
    1 cup (6 ounces) semisweet chocolate chips
    1 cup whipping cream
    1/4 cup sugar
    1/4 teaspoon ground cinnamon

In a mixing bowl, beat egg whites and vinegar on medium speed until foamy. Combine sugar and cinnamon; gradually beat into egg whites, 1 tablespoon at a time, on high until stiff peaks form. Spread into the pastry shell. Bake at 325° for 20-25 minutes or until meringue is lightly browned. Cool. For filling, whisk egg yolks and water in a saucepan. Add chocolate chips; cook and stir over low heat until a thermometer reads 160° and mixture is thickened (do not boil). Cool. Spread 3 tablespoons over meringue; set remainder aside. In a mixing bowl, beat the cream, sugar and cinnamon until stiff peaks form. Spread half over the chocolate layer. Fold remaining whipped cream into reserved chocolate mixture; spread over top. Chill for 6 hours or overnight. Refrigerate any leftovers. **Yield:** 8-10 servings.

Old-Fashioned Chess Pie

Christine Batts, Murray, Kentucky

This recipe dates back many years and has certainly stood the test of time. It's very rich, so small servings might be in order.

    1 cup butter (no substitutes), softened
    2 cups sugar
    6 egg yolks
    1 egg
    1/3 cup cornmeal
    1/4 cup all-purpose flour
    1/3 cup milk
    1 teaspoon vanilla extract
    1 unbaked deep-dish pastry shell (9 inches)

Custard, Pudding & Cream Pies

TOPPING:
    2 cups sugar, *divided*
    2/3 cup milk
    1/2 cup butter (no substitutes)

In a mixing bowl, cream butter and sugar. Beat in egg yolks and egg. Add the cornmeal and flour; mix well. Beat in milk and vanilla (do not overbeat). Pour into the pastry shell. Bake at 325° for 55-65 minutes or until the filling is almost set. Cool on a wire rack. In a heavy saucepan, heat 1/2 cup sugar over low heat without stirring until partially melted, about 5 minutes. Cook and stir with a metal spoon until syrup is completely melted and golden, about 5 minutes. Stir in milk, butter and remaining sugar (mixture will be lumpy). Cook over medium heat, stirring until a candy thermometer reads 234° (softball stage). Remove from the heat. Pour into a mixing bowl without stirring. Cool, without stirring, to 190°. Beat on high speed until mixture becomes light brown and creamy and a candy thermometer reads 130°-137°, about 5 minutes. Immediately spread over pie. Store in the refrigerator. **Yield:** 8-10 servings.

Southern Sweet Potato Pie

Bonnie Holcomb, Fulton, Mississippi

(Pictured above)

This recipe is very popular here in the South. It's a particular favorite at our house because we always have plenty of sweet potatoes in our garden. Try it with a dollop of whipped cream.

    3 tablespoons all-purpose flour
1-2/3 cups sugar
    1 cup mashed sweet potatoes
    2 eggs
    1/4 cup light corn syrup
    1/4 teaspoon ground nutmeg
Pinch salt

    1/2 cup butter *or* margarine
    3/4 cup evaporated milk
    1 unbaked pastry shell (9 inches)

In a large mixing bowl, combine the flour and sugar. Add sweet potatoes, eggs, corn syrup, nutmeg, salt, butter and evaporated milk; beat well. Pour into pastry shell. Bake at 350° for 55-60 minutes. Cool on a wire rack for 1 hour. Store in the refrigerator. **Yield:** 8 servings.

County Fair Pie

Judy Acuff, Lathrop, Missouri

(Pictured below)

This quick and easy recipe is one of my family's favorites. I've taken it to lots of potlucks and have been asked for the recipe many times.

    1/2 cup butter *or* margarine, melted
    1 cup sugar
    1/2 cup all-purpose flour
    2 eggs
    1 teaspoon vanilla extract
    1 cup coarsely chopped walnuts
    1 cup (6 ounces) semisweet chocolate chips
    1/2 cup butterscotch chips
    1 unbaked pastry shell (9 inches)

In a mixing bowl, beat the butter, sugar, flour, eggs and vanilla until well blended. Stir in nuts and chips. Pour into pastry shell. Bake at 325° for 1 hour or until golden brown. Cool on a wire rack for 1 hour. Store in the refrigerator. **Yield:** 6-8 servings.

1/4 teaspoon salt
1-3/4 cups water
1 cup raisins
1 tablespoon butter *or* margarine
2 teaspoons lemon juice
1 teaspoon grated lemon peel
1 pastry shell (9 inches), baked
1 cup (8 ounces) sour cream
1/4 cup confectioners' sugar
1/4 teaspoon ground nutmeg

In a small saucepan, combine the first five ingredients. Cook and stir until mixture comes to a boil and is thickened and bubbly. Remove from the heat; stir in the butter, lemon juice and peel. Cool for 5 minutes, stirring twice. Pour into pastry shell. Press a piece of plastic wrap over filling; refrigerate overnight. Remove plastic wrap. In a bowl, combine the sour cream, confectioners' sugar and nutmeg. Spread over filling. Store in the refrigerator. **Yield:** 6-8 servings.

Walnut Applesauce Pie

Mrs. F. Verbrugge, Franklin Lakes, New Jersey

(Pictured below)

My mother baked this pie every autumn, and it's become a tradition at our house. My husband always asks for seconds.

1 cup packed dark brown sugar
1/3 cup sugar
1 tablespoon all-purpose flour
1 egg plus 1 egg white
1/2 cup unsweetened applesauce
2 tablespoons milk
1 teaspoon vanilla extract
1 cup chopped walnuts
1 unbaked pastry shell (9 inches)
Whipped cream, optional

Strawberry Cheesecake Pie

Janis Plourde, Smooth Rock Falls, Ontario

(Pictured above)

This creamy concoction is so refreshing on a hot day and also really easy to assemble. With its appealing look, company will never know how simple it is.

2 cups sliced fresh strawberries
1/4 cup chopped almonds, toasted
1 tablespoon sugar
1 graham cracker crust (9 inches)
1 package (8 ounces) cream cheese, softened
2 cups cold milk, *divided*
1 package (3.4 ounces) instant vanilla pudding mix
Whipped cream, strawberry slices and fresh mint, optional

In a bowl, combine the strawberries, almonds and sugar. Pour into crust. In a mixing bowl, beat cream cheese until smooth; gradually add 1/2 cup of milk. Add pudding mix and remaining milk. Beat for 1 minute or until blended; pour over strawberries. Cover and refrigerate for 2 hours or until set. Garnish if desired. **Yield:** 8 servings.

Sour Cream Raisin Pie

Patricia Kile, Greentown, Pennsylvania

A hint of lemon gives zing to the creamy pudding-and-raisin filling in this homey dessert. Topped off with sweetened sour cream, it's sure to be a hit at your house.

1 package (3 ounces) cook-and-serve vanilla pudding mix
2 tablespoons sugar

Custard, Pudding & Cream Pies

In a mixing bowl, combine sugars and flour. Add egg, egg white, applesauce, milk and vanilla; mix well. Stir in walnuts. Pour into pastry shell. Bake at 375° for 40-45 minutes or until set. Cool on a wire rack for 1 hour. Store in the refrigerator. Serve with whipped cream if desired. **Yield:** 6-8 servings.

Orange Meringue Pie

June Nehmer, Las Vegas, Nevada

(Pictured above)

I found this recipe while vacationing in Florida in the late '60s. I made a few changes and added lime juice for extra tartness. It's colorful, refreshing and looks so pretty on the plate.

1-1/2 cups graham cracker crumbs (about 24 squares)
1/4 cup sugar
1/3 cup butter *or* margarine, melted
FILLING:
  1 cup sugar
  1/4 cup cornstarch
  1/4 teaspoon salt
  1 cup orange juice
  1/2 cup water
  3 egg yolks, well beaten
  2 tablespoons lime juice
  4 teaspoons grated orange peel
  1 tablespoon butter *or* margarine
MERINGUE:
  3 egg whites
  1/8 teaspoon cream of tartar
  6 tablespoons sugar

In a bowl, combine the cracker crumbs and sugar; stir in butter. Press onto the bottom and up the sides of a 9-in. pie plate. Bake at 375° for 8-10 minutes or until lightly browned. Cool. For filling, combine the sugar, cornstarch and salt in a saucepan. Whisk in orange juice and water until smooth. Cook and stir over medium heat until thickened and bubbly. Reduce heat; cook and stir 2 minutes longer. Remove from the heat. Gradually stir 1 cup hot filling into egg yolks; return all to the pan, stirring constantly. Bring to a gentle boil; cook and stir for 2 minutes. Remove from the heat; stir in the lime juice, orange peel and butter. Pour hot filling into pie crust. For the meringue, beat egg whites in a mixing bowl until foamy. Add cream of tartar; beat on medium speed until soft peaks form. Gradually beat in sugar, 1 tablespoon at a time, on high until stiff peaks form. Spread over hot filling, sealing edges to crust. Bake at 350° for 15 minutes or until golden brown. Cool on a wire rack for 1 hour; refrigerate for 1-2 hours before serving. Refrigerate leftovers. **Yield:** 6-8 servings.

Ambrosia Pecan Pie

Bernadine Stine, Roanoke, Indiana

Orange peel and coconut combine with pecans to make this truly special and rich-tasting dessert. It always wins compliments at Christmas dinner.

  3 eggs
  3/4 cup light corn syrup
  1/2 cup sugar
  3 tablespoons brown sugar
  3 tablespoons orange juice
  2 tablespoons butter *or* margarine, melted
  1 teaspoon grated orange peel
  1/8 teaspoon salt
1-1/2 cups chopped pecans
  2/3 cup flaked coconut
  1 unbaked pastry shell (9 inches)

In a large mixing bowl, beat eggs, corn syrup, sugars, orange juice, butter, orange peel and salt until well blended. Stir in pecans and coconut. Pour into pastry shell. Bake at 350° for 50-60 minutes or until a knife inserted near the center comes out clean. If edges become too brown, cover with foil. Cool on a wire rack for 1 hour. Store in the refrigerator. **Yield:** 8 servings.

Chocolate Banana Cream Pie

Jaquelin McTee, Eatonville, Washington

(Pictured at right and on p. 36)

My husband loves banana cream pie, and I like choco-late, so I combined the two in this doubly delicious pie. It's our favorite dessert, which means I get a lot of prac-tice making it!

- 1/2 cup sugar
- 1/4 cup cornstarch
- 1/4 teaspoon salt
- 1-1/2 cups milk
  - 1 cup whipping cream
  - 3 egg yolks, lightly beaten
  - 1 tablespoon butter *or* margarine
  - 2 teaspoons vanilla extract
  - 1 pastry shell (9 inches), baked
  - 4 squares (1 ounce *each*) semisweet chocolate, melted
  - 2 medium firm bananas, sliced
- Whipped cream and chocolate shavings, optional

In a saucepan, combine sugar, cornstarch and salt. Gradually add milk and cream until smooth. Cook and stir over medium-high heat until thickened and bubbly. Reduce heat; cook and stir 2 minutes more. Add a small amount to egg yolks; mix well. Return all to the pan. Bring to a gentle boil; cook and stir for 2 minutes. Re-move from the heat; stir in butter and vanilla. Pour half into the pastry shell; cover and refrigerate. Add choco-late to remaining custard; mix well. Cover and refriger-ate for 1 hour. Do not stir. Arrange bananas over filling. Carefully spoon chocolate custard over all. Refrigerate for at least 2 hours. Garnish with whipped cream and chocolate shavings if desired. **Yield:** 6-8 servings.

Walnut Mincemeat Pie

Laverne Kamp, Kutztown, Pennsylvania

As a cold and tasty finishing touch, my husband and I usually put a dip of vanilla ice cream on top of this pie. The recipe's from my mother—each year, I make it for Christmas, and then for my sister-in-law's New Year's party besides.

- 2 eggs
- 1 cup sugar
- 2 tablespoons all-purpose flour
- 1/8 teaspoon salt
- 2 cups prepared mincemeat
- 1/2 cup chopped walnuts
- 1/4 cup butter *or* margarine, melted
- 1 unbaked pastry shell (9 inches)

In a mixing bowl, lightly beat the eggs. Combine the sug-ar, flour and salt; gradually add to the eggs. Stir in the mincemeat, nuts and butter; pour into pastry shell. Bake

at 400° for 15 minutes. Reduce heat to 325°; bake 35-40 minutes longer or until a knife inserted near the center comes out clean. Cool completely. Store in the refrigerator. **Yield:** 6-8 servings.

Molasses Pumpkin Pie

Lois Fetting, Nelson, Wisconsin

For the last 40 years, our Thanksgiving feast has in-cluded roast goose or duck, hearty side dishes and this pie for dessert. It's a special old-fashioned treat. We love generous slices topped with whipped cream.

- Pastry for single-crust pie (9 inches)
  - 2 eggs
  - 1/2 cup sugar
  - 1 teaspoon ground cinnamon
  - 1/2 teaspoon salt
  - 1/2 teaspoon ground ginger
  - 1/2 teaspoon ground nutmeg
- 1-3/4 cups canned *or* cooked pumpkin
  - 3 tablespoons molasses
  - 3/4 cup evaporated milk
- Whipped topping

Line a 9-in. pie plate with pastry. Trim to 1/2 in. beyond edge of plate; flute edges. Set aside. In a mixing bowl, beat the eggs, sugar, cinnamon, salt, ginger and nut-meg. Beat in pumpkin and molasses; gradually add milk. Pour into crust. Cover edges loosely with foil. Bake at 425° for 10 minutes. Remove foil. Reduce heat to 350°; bake 28-32 minutes longer or until a knife inserted near the center comes out clean. Cool on a wire rack for 1-2 hours. Chill until serving. Serve with whipped top-ping. Refrigerate leftovers. **Yield:** 6-8 servings.

Dixie Pie

Sandra Pichon, Slidell, Louisiana

(Pictured below)

When Mom baked this old-fashioned sugar pie, family members would clamor for second servings. We love the combination of cinnamon, coconut, nuts and raisins. Thanksgiving and Christmas dinner were not complete without this dessert.

Pastry for two single-crust pies (9 inches)
1-1/2 cups raisins
    1 cup butter *or* margarine, softened
    1 cup sugar
    1 cup packed brown sugar
    6 eggs
    2 teaspoons vanilla extract
    2 to 4 teaspoons ground cinnamon
    1 cup chopped nuts
    1 cup flaked coconut
Whipped topping and additional chopped nuts, optional

Line two 9-in. pie plates with pastry. Trim pastry to 1/2 in. beyond edge of plate; flute edges. Line crusts with a double thickness of heavy-duty foil. Bake at 450° for 10 minutes. Remove foil. Cool on wire racks. Place raisins in a saucepan and cover with water; bring to a boil. Remove from the heat; set aside. In a mixing bowl, cream butter and sugars. Beat in eggs, vanilla and cinnamon until smooth. Drain raisins. Stir raisins, nuts and coconut into creamed mixture (mixture will appear curdled). Pour into the crusts. Bake at 350° for 30-35 minutes or until set. Cool on wire racks for 1 hour. Chill until serving. Garnish with whipped topping and additional chopped nuts if desired. **Yield: 2 pies (6-8 servings each).**

Grapefruit Meringue Pie

Barbara Soliday, Winter Haven, Florida

(Pictured above)

There's a grapefruit tree in our backyard, so I like to use fresh grapefruit juice when I make this pie. I just love the unique citrus flavor of this dessert.

1-1/3 cups sugar
    1/3 cup cornstarch
    2 cups pink grapefruit juice
    3/4 cup water
    3 egg yolks, lightly beaten
    2 tablespoons butter *or* margarine
    1/2 teaspoon lemon extract
    1 pastry shell (9 inches), baked
MERINGUE:
    3 egg whites
    1/4 teaspoon cream of tartar
    6 tablespoons sugar

In a saucepan, combine sugar and cornstarch. Gradually add grapefruit juice and water. Cook and stir over medium-high heat until thickened and bubbly, about 2 minutes. Reduce heat; cook and stir 2 minutes longer. Gradually stir 1/2 cup into egg yolks; return all to the pan. Bring to a gentle boil; cook and stir for 2 minutes. Remove from the heat; stir in butter and extract. Pour hot filling into pastry shell. In a mixing bowl, beat the egg whites and cream of tartar on medium speed until foamy. Gradually beat in sugar, 1 tablespoon at a time, on high just until stiff peaks form and sugar is dissolved. Spread meringue evenly over hot filling, sealing edges to crust. Bake at 350° for 15 minutes or until the meringue is golden brown. Cool on a wire rack for 1 hour. Refrigerate for at least 3 hours before serving. Store in the refrigerator. **Yield: 6-8 servings.**

Pecan Macadamia Pie

Anne Simboli, Farmville, Virginia

It's bound to be a blue-ribbon Christmas when I serve this rich, nutty pie—it was a prize-winner at our county fair. Even my husband, who can take or leave sweets, can't resist it!

    1 cup all-purpose flour
    2 tablespoons sugar
    1/2 teaspoon salt
    1/4 cup shortening
    3 to 4 tablespoons cold water
FILLING:
    3 eggs
    1/2 cup sugar
    4-1/2 teaspoons all-purpose flour
    1/4 teaspoon salt
    1 cup light corn syrup
    1 tablespoon butter *or* margarine, melted and
      cooled
    1 teaspoon vanilla extract
    1 cup coarsely chopped pecans
    3/4 cup coarsely chopped macadamia nuts

In a bowl, combine flour, sugar and salt; cut in shortening until crumbly. Gradually add cold water, tossing with a fork until dough forms a ball. On a lightly floured surface, roll out pastry to fit a 9-in. pie plate. Trim and flute edges. For filling, beat the eggs in a small mixing bowl until blended but not frothy. Add sugar, flour, salt and corn syrup; beat until smooth. Add butter and vanilla; mix just until blended. Stir in chopped pecans and macadamia nuts. Pour into crust. Bake at 325° for 55-60 minutes or until center is set. Cool on a wire rack for 1 hour. Store in the refrigerator. **Yield:** 8-10 servings.

Golden Squash Pie

Patricia Hardin, Seymour, Tennessee

Whether you take this yummy pie to a party or potluck dinner, be prepared to share the recipe. An alternative to the more traditional pumpkin pie, it bakes up high and flavorful.

    4 eggs
    4 cups mashed cooked butternut squash
    1 cup buttermilk
    1/4 cup butter *or* margarine, melted
    2 teaspoons vanilla extract
    2 cups sugar
    2 tablespoons all-purpose flour
    1 teaspoon salt
    1/2 teaspoon baking soda
    2 unbaked pastry shells (9 inches)
Ground nutmeg, optional

In a mixing bowl, combine the eggs, squash, buttermilk, butter and vanilla. Combine the dry ingredients; add to the squash mixture and mix until smooth. Pour into pas-

try shells. Cover edges loosely with foil. Bake at 350° for 35 minutes. Remove foil. Bake 25 minutes longer or until a knife inserted near the center comes out clean. Cool on wire racks for 1 hour. Sprinkle with nutmeg if desired. Store in the refrigerator. **Yield:** 2 pies (6-8 servings each).

Coconut Cream Pie

Vera Moffitt, Oskaloosa, Kansas

(Pictured below)

This is my own recipe for a pie that I make often. It's been a family-favorite dessert since the '40s, when I made several of these pies to serve a threshing crew of 21 hungry men! I guess you could say this creamy pie is a real crowd-pleaser.

    3/4 cup sugar
    3 tablespoons all-purpose flour
    1/8 teaspoon salt
    3 cups milk
    3 eggs, beaten
    1-1/2 cups flaked coconut, toasted, *divided*
    1 tablespoon butter *or* margarine
    1-1/2 teaspoons vanilla extract
    1 pastry shell (9 inches), baked

In a saucepan, combine sugar, flour and salt. Stir in milk until smooth; cook and stir over medium-high heat until thickened and bubbly. Cook and stir 2 minutes longer. Remove from the heat; gradually stir about 1 cup of hot mixture into beaten eggs. Return all to saucepan. Bring to a gentle boil. Cook and stir 2 minutes more. Remove from the heat; stir in 1 cup coconut, butter and vanilla. Pour into pastry shell; sprinkle with remaining coconut. Chill for several hours before serving. Refrigerate leftovers. **Yield:** 6-8 servings.

1 package (8 ounces) cream cheese,
  softened
1 cup sugar, *divided*
1/2 teaspoon salt
2 eggs
1/2 cup milk
1/2 teaspoon vanilla extract
1 tablespoon cornstarch
1 can (8 ounces) crushed pineapple,
  undrained
1 unbaked pastry shell (9 inches)
1/4 cup chopped pecans

In a mixing bowl, beat the cream cheese, 1/2 cup sugar and salt until smooth. Add eggs, one at a time, beating well after each addition. Beat in milk and vanilla; set aside. In a small saucepan, combine cornstarch and remaining sugar. Stir in pineapple; bring to a boil. Cook and stir 2 minutes or until thickened. Pour into pastry shell; spoon cream cheese mixture over top. Sprinkle with pecans. Bake at 400° for 10 minutes. Reduce heat to 325°; bake 45-50 minutes longer or until center is set. Cool on a wire rack for 1 hour. Chill before serving. **Yield:** 8 servings.

Peanut Butter Pie

Julianne Johnson, Grove City, Minnesota

(Pictured above)

This smooth creamy pie with a big peanut butter taste reminds me of Mom. It's sure to be a hit around your house, too. I like to make this dessert in the summer because it's simple to prepare and the kitchen stays cool.

2 packages (3 ounces *each*) cook-and-serve
  vanilla pudding mix
4 cups milk
1/2 cup creamy peanut butter
3/4 cup confectioners' sugar
1 pastry shell (9 inches), baked
Whipped cream

In a saucepan, cook pudding mixes and milk over medium heat until thickened and bubbly. Remove from the heat and cool slightly. Meanwhile, in a bowl, cut peanut butter into confectioners' sugar until mixture is crumbly. (Peanut butter consistency may vary; add additional confectioners' sugar if necessary.) Set aside 2 tablespoons of crumbs; sprinkle remaining mixture into pastry shell. Pour pudding over crumbs. Chill until set. Top with whipped cream; sprinkle with reserved crumbs. **Yield:** 6-8 servings.

Creamy Pineapple Pie

Priscilla Wortman, Belmont, Vermont

(Pictured at right)

A local radio station sponsored a contest that required recipes with three different products from the dairy case. I entered this recipe and won a prize!

Preventing Spills

To prevent a custard filling from spilling as you put the pie in the oven, pull out the oven rack a few inches, place the unfilled pastry shell on the rack, then pour in the filling. Carefully slide the rack back into its original position.

Lemon Meringue Pie

Susan Jones, Bradford, Ohio

(Pictured above)

My father loves lemon meringue pie and always wants one for his birthday. I rely on this recipe, which won first place at our county fair. It has a light flaky crust, refreshing lemon filling and soft meringue with pretty golden peaks.

1-1/2 cups all-purpose flour
  1/2 teaspoon salt
  1/2 cup shortening
  1/4 cup cold water
FILLING:
1-1/2 cups sugar
  1/4 cup cornstarch
    3 tablespoons all-purpose flour
  1/4 teaspoon salt
1-1/2 cups water
    3 egg yolks, beaten
    2 tablespoons butter *or* margarine
  1/3 cup lemon juice
    1 teaspoon grated lemon peel
    1 teaspoon lemon extract
MERINGUE:
    3 egg whites
  1/4 teaspoon cream of tartar
    6 tablespoons sugar

In a bowl, combine flour and salt; cut in shortening until crumbly. Gradually add water, tossing with a fork until a ball forms. Roll out pastry to fit a 9-in. pie plate. Transfer pastry to plate. Trim pastry to 1/2 in. beyond edge of plate; flute edges. Prick bottom and sides of pastry with a fork. Line with a double thickness of heavy-duty foil. Bake at 450° for 8 minutes. Remove foil; bake 5-6 minutes longer or until light golden brown. Reduce heat to 350°. For filling, combine sugar, cornstarch, flour and salt in a saucepan. Gradually stir in water. Cook and stir over medium-high heat until thickened and bubbly, about 2 minutes. Reduce the heat;

cook and stir 2 minutes longer. Remove from the heat. Gradually stir 1 cup hot filling into egg yolks; return all to pan. Bring to a gentle boil; cook and stir for 2 minutes. Remove from the heat. Stir in butter, lemon juice, peel and extract until butter is melted. Cover; set aside and keep hot. For meringue, beat egg whites and cream of tartar in a mixing bowl on medium speed until foamy, about 1 minute. Gradually beat in sugar, 1 tablespoon at a time, on high until stiff glossy peaks form and sugar is dissolved. Pour hot filling into crust. Spread meringue evenly over filling, sealing edges to crust. Bake at 350° for 15 minutes or until meringue is golden brown. Cool on a wire rack for 1 hour; refrigerate for at least 3 hours. Store in the refrigerator. **Yield:** 6-8 servings.

Butterscotch Pie

Cary Letsche, Bradenton, Florida

I highly recommend this pie for dessert. The thick custard topped with fluffy meringue makes a wonderful satisfying pie.

    6 tablespoons butter *or* margarine
    6 tablespoons all-purpose flour
1-1/2 cups packed brown sugar
    2 cups milk
  1/4 teaspoon salt
    3 eggs yolks, beaten
    1 teaspoon vanilla extract
    1 pastry shell (9 inches), baked
MERINGUE:
    3 egg whites
  1/4 teaspoon cream of tartar
  1/2 cup sugar

In a saucepan, melt the butter. Remove from the heat; stir in the flour until smooth. Stir in brown sugar. Return to heat; gradually add milk and salt, stirring constantly. Cook and stir over medium-high heat until thickened and bubbly. Reduce heat; cook and stir 2 minutes more. Remove from the heat. Stir about 1 cup into the egg yolks; return all to saucepan. Bring to a gentle boil. Cook and stir for 2 minutes. Remove from the heat and add vanilla. Pour into pastry shell. Immediately make the meringue: In a mixing bowl, beat egg whites and cream of tartar on medium until foamy, about 1 minute. Gradually beat in sugar, 1 tablespoon at a time, on high until stiff glossy peaks form and sugar is dissolved. Spread evenly over hot filling, sealing edges to crust. Bake at 350° for 15 minutes or until meringue is golden brown. Cool on a wire rack for 1 hour. Refrigerate for several hours or until chilled. Store in the refrigerator. **Yield:** 6-8 servings.

Double Peanut Pie

Vivian Cleeton, Richmond, Virginia

(Pictured below)

I created this recipe for a national pie contest and won second place for my state. Many peanuts are grown here, and I always look for ways to use local products.

    2 eggs
    1/3 cup creamy peanut butter
    1/3 cup sugar
    1/3 cup light corn syrup
    1/3 cup dark corn syrup
    1/3 cup butter *or* margarine, melted
    1 teaspoon vanilla extract
    1 cup salted peanuts
    1 unbaked pastry shell (9 inches)
Whipped cream *or* ice cream, optional

In a mixing bowl, beat the eggs; gradually add peanut butter, sugar, corn syrups, butter and vanilla; mix well. Fold in peanuts. Pour into the pastry shell. Bake at 375° for 30-35 minutes or until set. Cool on a wire rack for 1 hour. Store in the refrigerator. Serve with whipped cream or ice cream if desired. **Yield:** 6-8 servings.

Pineapple Coconut Pie

Elsie Wilson, Freeman, Missouri

(Pictured above)

My daughter introduced me to several recipes that are low in sugar after I found out I have diabetes. This was one of them, and it's become one of my favorite desserts.

    1 cup cold milk
    1 package (3.4 ounces) instant vanilla
      pudding mix
    1/2 cup flaked coconut
    1 can (8 ounces) crushed unsweetened
      pineapple, drained
    1 pastry shell (9 inches), baked
Whipped topping, optional

In a mixing bowl, beat milk and pudding mix on low speed for 2 minutes. Stir in the coconut and pineapple. Pour into pastry shell. Chill for at least 2 hours. Garnish with whipped topping if desired. **Yield:** 8 servings.

Chocolate Chip Pie

Ellen Benninger, Stoneboro, Pennsylvania

This dessert delights chocolate lovers and carries very well to a potluck dinner or other gathering.

    3 eggs
    3/4 cup sugar
    3/4 cup packed brown sugar
    3/4 cup all-purpose flour
    1/2 cup butter *or* margarine, melted and cooled
    1/4 cup vegetable oil
    1 teaspoon vanilla extract
1-1/2 cups semisweet chocolate chips
    1 cup chopped pecans *or* walnuts
    1 unbaked pastry shell (9 inches)

In a mixing bowl, beat eggs until foamy. Beat in sugars, flour, butter, oil and vanilla until well blended. Stir in chocolate chips and nuts. Pour into pastry shell. Bake at 325° for 1-1/4 hours or until a knife inserted near the center comes out clean. Cool on a wire rack for 1 hour. Chill until serving. Refrigerate leftovers. **Yield:** 8 servings.

Traditional Pumpkin Pie

Gloria Warczak, Cedarburg, Wisconsin

(Pictured below)

Usually I prepare two different desserts for our holiday dinner, but one of them must be pumpkin pie—otherwise, it just wouldn't seem like Thanksgiving. My version calls for more eggs than most, making this pie's pumpkin custard filling especially rich-tasting.

 2 cups all-purpose flour
 3/4 teaspoon salt
 2/3 cup shortening
 4 to 6 tablespoons cold water
FILLING:
 6 eggs
 1 can (29 ounces) solid-pack pumpkin
 2 cups packed brown sugar
 2 teaspoons ground cinnamon
 1 teaspoon salt
 1/2 teaspoon *each* ground cloves, nutmeg and
   ginger
 2 cups evaporated milk

In a bowl, combine flour and salt; cut in shortening until crumbly. Sprinkle with water, 1 tablespoon at a time, tossing with a fork until dough forms a ball. Divide dough in half. On a floured surface, roll out each portion to fit a 9-in. pie plate. Place pastry in plates; trim pastry (set scraps aside if leaf cutouts are desired) and flute edges. Set shells aside. For filling, beat eggs in a mixing bowl. Add pumpkin, sugar, cinnamon, salt, cloves, nutmeg and ginger; beat just until smooth. Gradually stir in milk. Pour into pastry shells. Bake at 450° for 10 minutes. Reduce heat to 350°; bake 40-45 minutes longer or until a knife inserted near the center comes out clean. Cool on wire racks. Store in the refrigerator. If desired, cut the pastry scraps with a 1-in. leaf-shaped cookie cutter; place on an ungreased baking sheet. Bake at 350° for 10-15 minutes or until lightly browned. Place on baked pies. **Yield:** 2 pies (6-8 servings each).

Coconut Banana Cream Pie

Tammy Olson, Bruce, South Dakota

(Pictured above)

After tasting it at a bake sale, I got the recipe for this pie from a friend, then adapted it. I make it for family gatherings—it's everyone's favorite treat—and also for when company comes by.

CRUST:
 3 cups flaked coconut
 7 tablespoons butter *or* margarine
FILLING:
 3/4 cup sugar
 1/4 cup all-purpose flour
 3 tablespoons cornstarch
 1/4 teaspoon salt
 3 cups half-and-half cream
 4 egg yolks, lightly beaten
 2 teaspoons vanilla extract
 2 large firm bananas, sliced
Whipped cream and sliced bananas, optional

In a skillet, saute coconut in butter until golden. Set aside 2 tablespoons for garnish. Press remaining coconut onto the bottom and up the sides of a greased 9-in. pie plate. Bake at 350° for 7 minutes. In a saucepan, combine the sugar, flour, cornstarch and salt. Gradually add cream. Cook and stir over medium-high heat until thickened and bubbly. Cook and stir for 2 minutes more. Add a small amount to egg yolks. Return all to pan. Bring to a gentle boil. Cook and stir for 2 minutes more. Remove from heat; add vanilla. Cool to room temperature. Place bananas in the crust. Cover with cream mixture. Chill until set, about 2 hours. Sprinkle with reserved coconut. If desired, garnish with whipped cream and bananas. **Yield:** 6-8 servings.

Custard, Pudding & Cream Pies

Old-Fashioned Chocolate Pie

Betsey Sue Halcott, Lebanon, Connecticut

Preparing this old-fashioned pie brings back a host of warm memories of time spent in the kitchen. When I was a young girl, we cranked homemade ice cream to serve with it.

      1/2 cup water
   1-1/2 squares (1-1/2 ounces) unsweetened
         baking chocolate
      1/4 cup butter (no substitutes)
      2/3 cup sugar
   1-1/2 teaspoons vanilla extract
FILLING:
      1/4 cup shortening
      3/4 cup sugar
        1 egg
        1 cup all-purpose flour
        1 teaspoon baking powder
      1/2 teaspoon salt
      1/2 cup milk
        1 unbaked pastry shell (9 inches)
        2 tablespoons chopped nuts, optional

In a saucepan, bring water, chocolate and butter to a boil; boil for 1 minute. Remove from the heat; add sugar and vanilla. Set aside. In a mixing bowl, cream shortening and sugar until light and fluffy. Add egg; beat well. Combine flour, baking powder and salt; add to creamed mixture alternately with milk. Pour into pastry shell. Carefully pour reserved chocolate mixture over filling. Sprinkle with chopped nuts if desired. Cover edges of pastry with foil. Bake at 350° for 55-60 minutes or until a toothpick inserted near the center comes out clean. Cool on a wire rack. Store in the refrigerator. **Yield:** 8 servings.

Lemon Blueberry Pie

Patricia Kile, Greentown, Pennsylvania

When fresh blueberries are in season, I find every way possible to enjoy them. This tart delicious pie proves the point! The lemon and blueberry flavors really complement each other.

        6 eggs, lightly beaten
        1 cup sugar
      1/2 cup butter *or* margarine
      1/3 cup lemon juice
        2 teaspoons grated lemon peel
        1 pastry shell (9 inches), baked
        3 cups fresh blueberries
      1/3 cup sugar
        1 tablespoon cornstarch
      1/4 cup orange juice

In a saucepan, combine eggs, sugar, butter, lemon juice and peel. Cook and stir over medium-low heat until thickened, about 20 minutes. Cool for 20 minutes, stir-

ring occasionally. Pour into pastry shell. In a saucepan, toss blueberries and sugar. Combine cornstarch and orange juice until smooth; add to blueberries. Bring to a boil over medium heat. Cook and stir for 2 minutes or until thickened. Cool for 15 minutes, stirring occasionally. Spoon over lemon layer. Chill for 4-6 hours. **Yield:** 8 servings.

Texas Lime Pie

Diane Bell, Manvel, Texas

(Pictured above)

With the perfect balance of sweet and tart, this velvety pie is a great way to beat the Texas heat and Gulf Coast humidity. With this simple recipe, even a novice cook can make a really memorable dessert. The recipe yields two pies, so you'll have enough to go around.

        3 cups graham cracker crumbs
      1/2 cup packed brown sugar
      2/3 cup butter *or* margarine, melted
        3 cans (14 ounces *each*) sweetened
          condensed milk
        5 egg yolks
        2 cups lime juice
Whipped topping, lime slices and fresh mint,
   optional

In a bowl, combine cracker crumbs, brown sugar and butter. Press onto the bottom and up the sides of two greased 9-in. pie plates. In a mixing bowl, beat milk, egg yolks and lime juice on low speed for 2 minutes or until smooth and slightly thickened. Pour into prepared crusts. Bake at 350° for 18-22 minutes or until a knife inserted near the center comes out clean. Cool on wire racks for 1 hour. Chill for 6 hours. Garnish with whipped topping, lime and mint if desired. **Yield:** 2 pies (6-8 servings each).

a mixing bowl. Add peels and salt; beat until smooth. In another bowl, beat eggs until thick and lemon-colored, about 5 minutes; slowly fold into ricotta mixture. Gently mix in remaining ingredients. Pour into the crust. Bake at 350° for 55 minutes or until a knife inserted near the center comes out clean. Cool on a wire rack for 1 hour. Store in the refrigerator. **Yield:** 6-8 servings.

Butterscotch Pumpkin Pie

Elizabeth Fehr, Cecil Lake, British Columbia

If you're tired of plain pumpkin pie, give this recipe a try. Convenient instant butterscotch pudding adds a tasty new twist. And the topping is the cream of the crop!

      1 cup graham cracker crumbs
  1/4 cup butter *or* margarine, melted
FILLING:
      1 cup cold milk
      1 package (3.4 ounces) instant butterscotch
        pudding mix
      1 cup cooked *or* canned pumpkin
      1 teaspoon ground cinnamon
  1/2 teaspoon ground nutmeg
TOPPING:
      1 cup whipped topping
      1 teaspoon vanilla extract

To make pie crust, combine crumbs and margarine; pat into a 9-in. pie plate. Bake at 350° for 10 minutes; cool. For filling, combine milk and pudding mix in a mixing bowl; beat well. Add pumpkin, cinnamon and nutmeg; mix well. Pour into crust. Chill for at least 2 hours. Combine topping ingredients; dollop on individual slices. **Yield:** 8 servings.

Maple Pecan Pie

Mildred Wescom, Belvidere, Vermont

(Pictured on p. 36)

Our Vermont maple syrup can't be beat, so I like to use it in a variety of recipes. This is one of my favorite pies using that sweet ingredient. It's also quick and easy to make.

      3 eggs
  1/2 cup sugar
      1 cup maple syrup
      3 tablespoons butter *or* margarine, melted
  1/2 teaspoon vanilla extract
  1/4 teaspoon salt
      1 cup pecan halves
      1 unbaked pastry shell (9 inches)

In a bowl, whisk eggs and sugar until smooth. Add maple syrup, butter, vanilla, salt and pecans. Pour into pastry shell. Bake at 375° for 40-45 minutes or until a knife inserted near the center comes out clean. Cool on a wire rack for 1 hour. Store in the refrigerator. **Yield:** 8 servings.

Easter Pie

Barbara Tierney, Farmington, Connecticut

(Pictured above)

Easter Pie is a specialty in many Italian homes, so mothers make sure their daughters master the recipe to ensure that the tradition continues.

CRUST:
1-2/3 cups all-purpose flour
      2 tablespoons sugar
  1/2 teaspoon salt
  1/4 teaspoon baking powder
  1/4 cup cold butter *or* margarine
  1/4 cup shortening
      2 eggs, lightly beaten
FILLING:
      1 carton (15 ounces) ricotta cheese
      1 cup sugar
      1 tablespoon all-purpose flour
  1/4 teaspoon grated lemon peel
  1/4 teaspoon grated orange peel
Dash salt
      4 eggs
      2 teaspoons vanilla extract
  1/3 cup semisweet chocolate chips
  1/3 cup diced citron, optional
  1/8 teaspoon ground cinnamon
Dash ground nutmeg

In a bowl, combine the flour, sugar, salt and baking powder; cut in butter and shortening until mixture resembles small crumbs. Add eggs; stir until moistened and mixture forms a ball. Cover and refrigerate for 1 hour. On a lightly floured surface, roll out dough to a 10-in. circle. Place in a 9-in. pie plate; flute crust. Refrigerate. For filling, beat the ricotta, sugar and flour in

Custard, Pudding & Cream Pies

Frosted Orange Pie

Delores Edgecomb, Atlanta, New York

(Pictured below)

I discovered the recipe for this distinctive pie in a very old church cookbook. With its fresh-tasting filling and fluffy frosting, it's truly an elegant final course.

    3/4 cup sugar
    1/2 cup all-purpose flour
    1/4 teaspoon salt
    1-1/4 cups water
      2 egg yolks, lightly beaten
      2 to 3 tablespoons grated orange peel
    1/2 teaspoon grated lemon peel
    1/2 cup orange juice
      2 tablespoons lemon juice
      1 pastry shell (9 inches), baked
    FROSTING:
    1/2 cup sugar
      2 egg whites
      2 tablespoons water
    1/8 teaspoon cream of tartar
    1/8 teaspoon salt
    1/2 cup flaked coconut, toasted, optional
    Orange slices and fresh mint, optional

In a saucepan, combine sugar, flour and salt; gradually add water. Cook and stir over medium-high heat for 2 minutes or until thickened and bubbly. Reduce heat; cook and stir 2 minutes longer. Remove from heat. Gradually stir 1/2 cup into egg yolks; return all to pan. Bring to a gentle boil; cook and stir for 2 minutes. Remove from the heat; stir in orange and lemon peel. Gently stir in juices. Pour into pastry shell. Cool on a wire rack for 1 hour. Chill at least 3 hours. In a heavy saucepan or double boiler, combine sugar, egg whites, water, cream of tartar and salt. With a portable mixer, beat on low speed for 1 minute. Continue beating on low over low

heat until frosting reaches 160°, about 8-10 minutes. With a stand mixer, beat on high until frosting forms stiff peaks, about 7 minutes. Spread over chilled pie. Just before serving, sprinkle with coconut if desired. Store in the refrigerator. Garnish with orange slices and mint if desired. **Yield:** 6-8 servings.

Banana Cream Pie

Bernice Morris, Marshfield, Missouri

(Pictured above)

Made from our farm-fresh dairy products, this pie was a sensational creamy treat anytime that Mom served it. Her recipe is a real treasure, and I've never found one that tastes better!

    3/4 cup sugar
    1/3 cup all-purpose flour
    1/4 teaspoon salt
      2 cups milk
      3 egg yolks, lightly beaten
      2 tablespoons butter *or* margarine
      1 teaspoon vanilla extract
      1 pastry shell (9 inches), baked
      3 medium firm bananas
    Whipped cream and additional sliced bananas

In a saucepan, combine sugar, flour and salt; stir in milk and mix well. Cook and stir over medium-high heat until the mixture is thickened and bubbly. Cook and stir for 2 minutes longer. Remove from the heat. Stir a small amount into egg yolks; return all to saucepan. Bring to a gentle boil. Cook and stir for 2 minutes; remove from the heat. Add butter and vanilla; cool slightly. Slice the bananas into pastry shell; pour filling over top. Cool on wire rack for 1 hour. Store in the refrigerator. Before serving, garnish with whipped cream and bananas. **Yield:** 6-8 servings.

Buttermilk Raisin Pie

John Ferren, Paris, Tennessee

(Pictured below)

Buttermilk is as common in the South as iced tea. This old-fashioned pie is just another fine way to cook with it. It's one of my favorites.

1-1/2 cups sugar
6 tablespoons cornstarch
1/4 teaspoon salt
3 cups buttermilk
3 egg yolks
3 tablespoons lemon juice
1 tablespoon butter *or* margarine
1 teaspoon vanilla extract
3/4 cup raisins
1 pastry shell (9 inches), baked
MERINGUE:
3 egg whites
1/4 teaspoon cream of tartar
6 tablespoons sugar

In a saucepan, combine sugar, cornstarch and salt. Stir in buttermilk until smooth. Cook and stir over medium-high heat until thickened and bubbly. Reduce heat; cook and stir 2 minutes more. Remove from the heat; stir in lemon juice, butter and vanilla. Stir in raisins. Pour into pastry shell. For meringue, beat egg whites and cream of tartar in a mixing bowl until soft peaks form. Gradually add sugar, beating until stiff peaks form. Spread over hot filling, sealing edges to crust. Bake at 350° for 15 minutes or until lightly browned. Cool on a wire rack for 1 hour. Refrigerate for at least 3 hours before serving. Store in the refrigerator. **Yield:** 6-8 servings.

Cream Puff Pie

Holly Camozzi, Rohnert Park, California

(Pictured above and on p. 36)

When I was a girl, my mother, sister and I made mini cream puffs. Now, instead of several little puffs, I make one big pie for big appetites. Since we're dairy farmers, it's doubly popular!

CRUST:
1/2 cup water
1/4 cup butter (no substitutes)
1/2 teaspoon salt
1/2 cup all-purpose flour
2 eggs
FILLING:
3/4 cup sugar
1/3 cup all-purpose flour
1/8 teaspoon salt
2 cups milk
2 eggs, lightly beaten
1 teaspoon vanilla extract
2 cups whipped cream, *divided*
Chocolate sauce and fresh raspberries, optional

In a large saucepan, bring water, butter and salt to a boil. Add flour all at once and stir until a smooth ball forms. Remove from the heat; let stand for 5 minutes. Add eggs, one at a time, beating well after each addition. Continue beating until mixture is smooth and shiny. Spread onto the bottom and halfway up the sides of a well-greased 9-in. pie plate. Bake at 400° for 35-40 minutes. Cool completely. For filling, combine sugar, flour and salt. Stir in milk until smooth. Cook and stir over medium-high heat until thickened and bubbly. Reduce heat; cook and stir 2 minutes more. Remove from the heat. Stir a small amount into egg yolks; return all to saucepan. Bring to a gentle boil. Cook and stir for 2 minutes more. Stir in vanilla. Cool. Fold in 1 cup of whipped cream. Pour into the crust. Top with remaining whipped cream. Chill for 2 hours. Garnish with chocolate sauce and raspberries if desired. **Yield:** 6-8 servings.

Praline Pumpkin Pie

Sandra Haase, Baltimore, Maryland

For me, baking is a relaxation rather than a chore. This is one of my favorites, a dessert I adapted from a neighbor's recipe for praline chocolate pie.

     1/3 cup finely chopped pecans
     1/3 cup packed brown sugar
       3 tablespoons butter *or* margarine,
          softened
       1 unbaked pastry shell (10 inches)
FILLING:
       3 eggs, lightly beaten
     1/2 cup sugar
     1/2 cup packed brown sugar
       2 tablespoons all-purpose flour
     3/4 teaspoon ground cinnamon
     1/2 teaspoon salt
     1/2 teaspoon ground ginger
     1/4 teaspoon ground cloves
       1 can (15 ounces) solid-pack pumpkin
   1-1/2 cups half-and-half cream
Additional chopped pecans, optional

Combine the pecans, sugar and butter; press onto the bottom of pastry shell. Prick sides of pastry with a fork. Bake at 450° for 10 minutes; cool for 5 minutes. In a mixing bowl, combine first eight filling ingredients; stir in pumpkin. Gradually add cream. Pour into pastry shell. If desired, sprinkle chopped pecans over top. Bake at 350° for 45-50 minutes or until a knife inserted near the center comes out clean. Cool on a wire rack for 1 hour. Store in the refrigerator. **Yield:** 8 servings.

German Chocolate Pie

Cheryl Jacobson, Chino Valley, Arizona

I'm known among family and friends for my desserts. This one is their very favorite. It's been a sweet standby of mine for some 25 years now.

       1 package (4 ounces) German sweet chocolate
     1/4 cup butter (no substitutes)
       1 can (12 ounces) evaporated milk
   1-1/2 cups sugar
       3 tablespoons cornstarch
     1/8 teaspoon salt
       2 eggs, lightly beaten
       1 teaspoon vanilla extract
       1 unbaked deep-dish pastry shell (9 inches)
     1/2 cup chopped pecans
   1-1/3 cups flaked coconut

In a saucepan, melt chocolate and butter over low heat; stir until blended. Remove from the heat and grad-

ually stir in milk; set aside. In a bowl, combine sugar, cornstarch and salt. Stir in eggs and vanilla. Gradually stir in chocolate mixture. Pour into pastry shell. Combine pecans and coconut; sprinkle over filling. Bake at 375° for 45-50 minutes or until puffed and browned. Cool on a wire rack for 1-2 hours. Chill (filling will become firm as it cools). **Yield:** 6-8 servings.

Black Forest Pie

Trudy Black, Dedham, Massachusetts

(Pictured below)

With three active children, I don't usually fuss with fancy desserts. This one is simple but impressive—it's the one I make to show how much I care. The tempting combination of chocolate and tangy red cherries is guaranteed to make someone feel special.

     3/4 cup sugar
     1/3 cup baking cocoa
       2 tablespoons all-purpose flour
     1/3 cup milk
     1/4 cup butter *or* margarine, cubed
       2 eggs, lightly beaten
       1 can (21 ounces) cherry pie filling, *divided*
       1 unbaked pastry shell (9 inches)
Whipped topping, optional

In a saucepan, combine sugar, cocoa, flour and milk until smooth. Add butter. Bring to a boil; cook and stir for 2 minutes or until thickened. Remove from the heat. Stir a small amount of hot mixture into eggs. Return all to the pan. Fold in half of the pie filling. Pour into pastry shell. Bake at 350° for 35-40 minutes or until filling is almost set. Cool completely on a wire rack. Just before serving, top with remaining pie filling and whipped topping if desired. Store in the refrigerator. **Yield:** 6-8 servings.

Shamrock Pie

Gloria Warczak, Cedarburg, Wisconsin

(Pictured at right)

Guests may wonder if the dessert has been touched by a leprechaun when they see the green layer in my lemon meringue pie. Then, after their first taste, they tell me they feel lucky to be enjoying such a dessert! Don't save it for just St. Patrick's Day, though. It's great the rest of the year, too.

- 1 cup sugar
- 1/4 cup cornstarch
- 1-1/2 cups water
- 3 egg yolks, lightly beaten
- 1/4 cup lemon juice
- 1 tablespoon butter *or* margarine
- 1-1/2 teaspoons grated lemon peel
- 5 to 6 drops green food coloring
- 1 pastry shell (9 inches), baked

MERINGUE:
- 3 egg whites
- 1/3 cup sugar

Combine the sugar, cornstarch and water in a saucepan; stir until smooth. Cook and stir over medium-high heat until thickened and bubbly. Reduce heat; cook and stir 2 minutes more. Stir a small amount into egg yolks; return all to the pan. Bring to a gentle boil. Cook and stir 2 minutes more. Remove from heat; stir in the lemon juice, butter, lemon peel and food coloring. Pour into the pastry shell. For meringue, beat the egg whites until foamy. Gradually add sugar and beat until stiff peaks form. Spread over hot filling, sealing edges to crust. Bake at 350° for 15 minutes or until lightly brown. Cool on a wire rack for 1 hour. Refrigerate for at least 3 hours before serving. Store in the refrigerator. **Yield:** 6-8 servings.

Crustless Pumpkin Pie

Thelia Busse, Cresco, Pennsylvania

Have all the flavor of a pumpkin pie without the fuss of making a crust with this easy recipe. It's a tasty way to celebrate the season.

- 1 can (15 ounces) solid-pack pumpkin
- 1 can (12 ounces) evaporated milk
- 2 eggs
- 2 egg whites
- 3/4 cup sugar
- 1 teaspoon ground cinnamon
- 1/4 teaspoon ground allspice
- 1/4 teaspoon ground ginger
- 1/8 teaspoon salt
- 1/2 cup graham cracker crumbs

Whipped topping and additional cinnamon, optional

In a mixing bowl, combine the pumpkin, milk, eggs, egg whites and sugar; beat until smooth. Add the spices and salt; beat until well mixed. Stir in graham cracker crumbs. Pour into a greased 9-in. pie plate. Bake at 325° for 50-55 minutes or until a knife inserted near the center comes out clean. Cool on a wire rack for 1 hour. Store in the refrigerator. Garnish with whipped topping and sprinkle with cinnamon if desired. **Yield:** 8 servings.

Poor Man's Pecan Pie

Fay Harrington, Seneca, Missouri

This is a recipe my mother-in-law shared with me several years ago. It's easy to make, and most of the ingredients are in everybody's cupboard. And it does really taste like pecan pie. We have it quite often, but it's tradition to have this pie on the menu during the holidays.

- 3 eggs
- 1 cup sugar
- 1 cup old-fashioned oats
- 3/4 cup dark corn syrup
- 1/2 cup flaked coconut
- 2 tablespoons butter *or* margarine, melted
- 1 teaspoon vanilla extract
- 1 unbaked pastry shell (9 inches)

Whipped topping and toasted coconut, optional

In a bowl, combine the first seven ingredients; mix well. Pour into pastry shell. Bake at 375° for 15 minutes; reduce heat to 350°. Bake 30-35 minutes longer or until a knife inserted near the center comes out clean. If necessary, cover edges of crust with foil to prevent over-browning. Cool on a wire rack for 1 hour. Store in the refrigerator. Garnish with whipped topping and toasted coconut if desired. **Yield:** 8-10 servings.

Lemon Supreme Pie

Jana Beckman, Wamego, Kansas

(Pictured below and on p. 36)

A friend and I often visit a local restaurant for pie and coffee. When they stopped carrying our favorite, I got busy in the kitchen and created this version, which we think tastes even better! The combination of the cream cheese and tart lemon is wonderful.

1 unbaked deep-dish pastry shell (9 inches)
LEMON FILLING:
1-1/2 cups sugar, *divided*
    6 tablespoons cornstarch
1/2 teaspoon salt
1-1/4 cups water
    2 tablespoons butter *or* margarine
    2 teaspoons grated lemon peel
    4 to 5 drops yellow food coloring,
      optional
2/3 cup lemon juice
CREAM CHEESE FILLING:
    2 packages (one 8 ounces, one 3 ounces)
      cream cheese, softened
3/4 cup confectioners' sugar
1-1/2 cups whipped topping
    1 tablespoon lemon juice

Line unpricked pastry shell with a double thickness of heavy-duty foil. Bake at 450° for 8 minutes. Remove foil; bake 5 minutes longer. Cool on a wire rack. In a saucepan, combine 3/4 cup sugar, cornstarch and salt. Stir in water; bring to a boil over medium-high heat. Reduce heat; add the remaining sugar. Cook and stir for 2 minutes or until thickened and bubbly. Remove from the heat; stir in butter, lemon peel and food coloring if desired. Gently stir in lemon juice (do not overmix). Cool to room temperature, about 1 hour. In a mixing bowl, beat cream cheese and sugar until smooth. Fold in whipped topping and lemon juice. Refrigerate 1/2 cup

for garnish. Spread remaining cream cheese mixture into pastry shell; top with lemon filling. Chill overnight. Place reserved cream cheese mixture in a pastry bag with a #21 star tip; pipe stars onto pie. Store in the refrigerator. **Yield:** 6-8 servings.

Raisin Custard Pie

Ruth Ann Stelfox, Raymond, Alberta

(Pictured above)

A comforting, old-fashioned dessert, this custard pie is one of my mom's best. The fluffy meringue makes it look so special, and the raisins are a nice surprise.

1/2 cup sugar
    3 tablespoons cornstarch
    2 cups milk
    3 egg yolks
    2 teaspoons lemon juice
1/2 cup raisins
    1 pastry shell (9 inches), baked
MERINGUE:
    3 egg whites
1/4 cup sugar

In a saucepan, combine sugar and cornstarch. Stir in milk until smooth. Cook and stir over medium-high heat until thickened and bubbly. Reduce heat; cook and stir 2 minutes more. Remove from the heat. Stir a small amount of hot filling into yolks. Return all to pan. Bring to a gentle boil. Cook and stir for 2 minutes more. Remove from the heat. Add lemon juice and raisins. Pour into pastry shell. For meringue, beat egg whites in a small bowl until foamy. Gradually add sugar, about 1 tablespoon at a time, beating until stiff and glossy. Spread over hot filling, sealing edges to crust. Bake at 350° for 15 minutes or until golden brown. Cool on a wire rack for 1 hour. Serve warm or cold. Store leftovers in the refrigerator. **Yield:** 8 servings. **Variation:** Cool filling in crust completely, then refrigerate. Just before serving, top with whipped cream instead of meringue.

Quick Coconut Cream Pie

Betty Claycomb, Alverton, Pennsylvania

(Pictured above)

I've found a way to make coconut cream pie without a lot of fuss and still get terrific flavor. Using a convenient purchased crust, instant pudding and frozen whipped topping, I can enjoy an old-time dessert even when time is short.

1-1/2 cups cold milk
1 package (5.1 ounces) instant vanilla
    pudding mix
1 carton (8 ounces) frozen whipped topping,
    thawed, *divided*
3/4 to 1 cup flaked coconut, toasted,
    divided
1 pastry shell, baked *or* graham cracker
    crust (8 *or* 9 inches)

In a mixing bowl, beat milk and pudding mix on low speed for 2 minutes. Fold in half of the whipped topping and 1/2 to 3/4 cup of coconut. Pour into crust. Spread with remaining whipped topping; sprinkle with remaining coconut. Chill. **Yield:** 6-8 servings.

Raspberry Cream Meringue Pie

Karen Rempel Arthur, Wainfleet, Ontario

(Pictured at right)

Whether my husband and I are hosting a backyard barbecue or a formal dinner, we love treating guests to this raspberry pie. I transport it to potlucks or family gath-

erings in my extra-deep cake carrier so the meringue stays intact.

1/3 cup plus 1/4 cup sugar, *divided*
3 tablespoons cornstarch
1-1/2 cups milk
4 eggs, *separated*
1 teaspoon butter *or* margarine
1/4 teaspoon almond extract
1 graham cracker crust (10 inches)
1-1/8 teaspoons unflavored gelatin
2 tablespoons plus 1/4 teaspoon cold water,
    divided
1 can (21 ounces) raspberry pie filling
3/4 teaspoon cream of tartar

In a saucepan, combine 1/3 cup sugar and cornstarch. Stir in milk until smooth. Cook and stir over medium-high heat until thickened and bubbly. Reduce heat; cook and stir 2 minutes longer. Remove from the heat. Stir a small amount of mixture into egg yolks. Return all to the pan, stirring constantly. Bring to a gentle boil; cook and stir 2 minutes more. Remove from the heat; stir in butter and extract. Pour hot filling into the crust. Sprinkle gelatin over 2 tablespoons cold water; let stand for 2 minutes. In a saucepan, bring raspberry filling and gelatin mixture to a boil. Reduce heat; simmer, uncovered, for 5 minutes. Meanwhile, in a mixing bowl, beat egg whites and cream of tartar on medium speed until soft peaks form. Beat in remaining water. Gradually beat in remaining sugar on high until stiff glossy peaks form and sugar is dissolved. Pour hot raspberry filling over custard. Spread meringue evenly over hot filling, sealing edges to crust. Bake at 350° for 15 minutes or until meringue is golden. Cool on a wire rack for 1 hour. Refrigerate for at least 3 hours before serving. Refrigerate leftovers. **Yield:** 8-10 servings.

Custard, Pudding & Cream Pies

Tropical Fruit Cream Pie

Carolyn Dixon, Monticello, Arkansas

I use crunchy toasted coconut to add a special touch to this sweet and creamy pie. It can be stirred up in a jiffy with handy pantry staples. With this fruity pie, you can treat your family to a taste of the tropics without even leaving your home!

- 2 cups cold milk
- 1 package (3.4 ounces) instant coconut cream pudding mix
- 1 can (15-1/4 ounces) tropical fruit salad, drained
- 1/2 cup flaked coconut, toasted
- 1 graham cracker crust (9 inches)

In a mixing bowl, beat milk and pudding mix on low speed for 2 minutes. Let stand until slightly thickened, about 2 minutes. Stir in the fruit and coconut. Pour into the graham cracker crust. Refrigerate until serving. **Yield:** 6-8 servings.

Chocolate Cream Cheese Pie

Rhonda Hogan, Eugene, Oregon

This impressive pie only looks like you fussed. In fact, it's quick and easy to prepare. Sometimes I add finely chopped pecans to the pudding layer to add a little texture. Either way, my family gobbles it up as fast as I make it.

- 1 package (3 ounces) cream cheese, softened
- 2 tablespoons sugar
- 1-3/4 cups cold milk, *divided*
- 3-1/2 cups whipped topping, *divided*
- 1 graham cracker crust (8 *or* 9 inches)
- 1 package (3.9 ounces) instant chocolate pudding mix

Miniature semisweet chocolate chips, optional

In a small mixing bowl, beat the cream cheese, sugar and 1 tablespoon milk until smooth. Gently stir in 1 cup whipped topping. Spread evenly into the graham cracker crust. In a large mixing bowl, beat pudding mix and remaining milk on low speed for 2 minutes. Pour over the top of the cream cheese mixture. Refrigerate until serving. Garnish with remaining whipped topping and chocolate chips if desired. **Yield:** 6 servings.

Old-Fashioned Custard Pie

Maxine Linkenauger, Montverde, Florida

(Pictured below)

This recipe came from the best cook in West Virginia— my mother! I just added a little to her ingredients. I'm a widow, and my grown children live in another state. So mostly I make my custard pie for church and club functions. It's the most different pie of all the ones in my recipe collection.

- Pastry for single- or double-crust pie* (9 inches)
- 4 eggs
- 2-1/2 cups milk
- 1/2 cup sugar
- 1 teaspoon vanilla extract
- 1 teaspoon almond extract
- 1 teaspoon salt
- 1 teaspoon ground nutmeg

Line a 9-in. pie plate with bottom pastry; flute edges or prepare a braided crust (see Editor's Note). Bake at 400° for 10 minutes. Meanwhile, beat eggs in a large bowl. Add remaining ingredients; mix well. Pour into crust. Cover edges with foil. Bake for 20-25 minutes or until a knife inserted near the center comes out clean. Cool completely. Store in the refrigerator. **Yield:** 6-8 servings. ***Editor's Note:** Pastry for a double crust is needed only if a braided crust is desired. To prepare braided crust: Trim pastry even with the edge of the pie plate; brush with water. From the top pastry, cut 12 strips, each 1/4 in. thick. Using three strips at a time, braid pastry on edge of crust, attaching ends together. Press down gently. Bake as directed above.

p. 64

p. 66

p. 70

p. 70

p. 72

Cool Refrigerator Pies

FROM THE FRIDGE. Clockwise from upper left: Tin Roof Fudge Pie (p. 64), Summer Berry Cheese Pie (p. 70), Banana Cream Cheese Pie (p. 66), Fluffy Caramel Pie (p. 70) and White Chocolate Berry Pie (p. 72).

with whipped cream and peanuts if desired. For topping, in a small saucepan over low heat, melt the caramels, cream and butter. Drizzle over the pie. Refrigerate until serving. **Yield:** 8-10 servings. ***Editor's Note:** This recipe was tested with Hershey caramels.

Candy Bar Pie

Mary Ann Smith, Groton, New York

(Pictured below)

Here's a very rich and creamy pie that tastes terrific. A small sliver is all most folks can handle. But that never stops anyone from asking for the recipe, or asking me to make it for more gatherings!

　　5 Snickers candy bars (2.07 ounces *each*),
　　　　cut into 1/4-inch pieces
　　1 pastry shell (9 inches), baked
　　12 ounces cream cheese, softened
　　1/2 cup sugar
　　2 eggs
　　1/3 cup sour cream
　　1/3 cup peanut butter
　　2/3 cup semisweet chocolate chips
　　2 tablespoons whipping cream

Place candy bar pieces in the pastry shell; set aside. In a mixing bowl, beat cream cheese and sugar until smooth. Add eggs, sour cream and peanut butter; beat on low speed just until combined. Pour into pastry shell. Bake at 325° for 35-40 minutes or until set. Cool on a wire rack. In a small heavy saucepan, melt chocolate chips with cream over low heat; stir until smooth. Spread over filling. Refrigerate for 2 hours or overnight. Cut with a warm knife. **Yield:** 8-10 servings.

Tin Roof Fudge Pie

Cynthia Kolberg, Syracuse, Indiana

(Pictured above and on p. 62)

This delectable pie makes a great hostess gift for a holiday get-together or a wonderful ending to a meal for company. No one can ever resist the rich chocolate filling with a peanutty layer.

　　2 squares (1 ounce *each*) semisweet chocolate
　　1 tablespoon butter (no substitutes)
　　1 pastry shell (9 inches), baked
PEANUT LAYER:
　　20 caramels*
　　1/3 cup whipping cream
1-1/2 cups salted peanuts
CHOCOLATE LAYER:
　　8 squares (1 ounce *each*) semisweet chocolate
　　2 tablespoons butter (no substitutes)
　　1 cup whipping cream
　　2 teaspoons vanilla extract
Whipped cream and salted peanuts, optional
TOPPING:
　　3 caramels
　　5 teaspoons whipping cream
　　1 tablespoon butter (no substitutes)

In a microwave, melt the chocolate and butter. Spread onto the bottom and up the sides of pastry shell; refrigerate until the chocolate is set. For peanut layer, in a saucepan over low heat, melt caramels and whipping cream, stirring frequently until smooth. Remove from the heat; stir in peanuts. Spoon into pastry shell; refrigerate. For chocolate layer, in a small saucepan over low heat, melt the chocolate and butter. Remove from the heat; let stand 15 minutes. Meanwhile, in a small mixing bowl, beat whipping cream and vanilla until soft peaks form. Carefully fold a third of the whipped cream into the chocolate mixture; fold in the remaining whipped cream. Spread over peanut layer; refrigerate until set. Garnish

Cherry Banana Cream Pie

Denise Elder, Hanover, Ontairo

This pretty pie's crunchy crust is spread with a rich butter layer, then topped with a fluffy filling flavored with banana, cherries and chocolate. Guests always tell me that this dreamy dessert reminds them of a banana split...and then ask for seconds.

3/4 cup butter *or* margarine, softened, *divided*
2 cups crushed vanilla wafers (about 60)
3/4 cup confectioners' sugar
FILLING:
  1 cup whipping cream
1/4 cup sugar
  2 tablespoons baking cocoa
  1 cup chopped walnuts
  1 large firm banana, thinly sliced
1/3 cup halved maraschino cherries
Whipped topping, chocolate curls and additional
  maraschino cherries

Melt 1/2 cup of butter; toss with wafer crumbs. Press into a 9-in. pie plate. In a small mixing bowl, cream the remaining butter; beat in confectioners' sugar until combined. Spread over crust. In another mixing bowl, beat the cream, sugar and cocoa until stiff peaks form. Fold in the walnuts, banana and maraschino cherries. Spoon into crust. Cover and refrigerate for 8 hours or overnight. Garnish with whipped topping, chocolate curls and cherries. **Yield:** 6-8 servings.

Chocolate Mint Cream Pie

Donna Christopher, Crestwood, Missouri

This light and refreshing pie is an ideal way to give your holiday guests a sweet treat without going through a lot of fuss in the kitchen. What's more, it cuts nicely, making it a cinch to serve.

  2 cups crushed chocolate-covered mint
    cookies
  3 to 4 tablespoons hot water
  1 graham cracker crust (8 inches)
  1 package (3 ounces) cream cheese,
    softened
1/3 cup sugar
  2 tablespoons milk
1/4 teaspoon peppermint extract
  1 carton (8 ounces) frozen whipped
    topping, thawed
  6 to 10 drops green food coloring, optional

Set aside 2 tablespoons cookie crumbs for garnish. In a bowl, combine remaining cookie crumbs with enough hot water to make crumbs spreadable. Spoon over the graham cracker crust; spread out evenly. Set aside. In a mixing bowl, beat cream cheese until fluffy. Add the sugar, milk and peppermint extract; beat until smooth. Fold in whipped topping. If food coloring is desired, di-

vide mixture in half and add coloring to one half. Alternately spoon mounds of plain and colored mixture into crust; swirl with a knife. Sprinkle with reserved cookie crumbs. Cover and refrigerate for 3 hours or until firm. **Yield:** 8-10 servings.

Peach Mallow Pie

Judie Anglen, Riverton, Wyoming

(Pictured above)

Marshmallows give a nice light texture to this versatile pie. I've made it with strawberries or raspberries, too. You can even substitute grated chocolate bars for the fruit. This dessert is a breeze to make ahead and keep in the refrigerator.

  35 large marshmallows
1/2 cup milk
1-1/2 cups frozen sliced peaches, thawed *or* 1
    package (10 ounces) frozen sweetened
    raspberries, thawed, undrained
1/8 teaspoon almond extract
  1 carton (8 ounces) frozen whipped
    topping, thawed
  1 graham cracker crust (9 inches)

Place marshmallows and milk in a large microwave-safe bowl. Microwave, uncovered, on high for 1-2 minutes. Stir until smooth; set aside. Finely chop the peaches; mash lightly with a fork or pulse in a food processor until finely chopped. Add to marshmallow mixture. Stir in the almond extract. Fold in the whipped topping; pour into graham cracker crust. Refrigerate for 2 hours. **Yield:** 6-8 servings. **Editor's Note:** This recipe was tested in an 850-watt microwave.

No-Bake Cheesecake Pie

Geneva Mayer, Olney, Illinois

I came up with this creamy white chocolate cheesecake after remembering one evening that I needed to bring a treat to the office the next day. It was a tremendous hit. It's quick to fix yet tastes like you fussed.

- 1 cup vanilla *or* white chips
- 2 packages (8 ounces *each*) cream cheese, cubed
- 1 carton (8 ounces) frozen whipped topping, thawed
- 1 graham cracker crust (9 inches)
- 1/3 cup English toffee bits *or* almond brickle chips

In a heavy saucepan, melt vanilla chips over medium-low heat; stir until smooth. Remove from the heat; stir in cream cheese until smooth. Fold in whipped topping. Pour into the crust. Cover and refrigerate overnight or until set. Just before serving, sprinkle with toffee bits. **Yield:** 6-8 servings.

Blackberry Breeze Pie

Gail Toepfer, Iron Ridge, Wisconsin

Making dessert doesn't necessarily require heating up your kitchen. This fluffy no-bake treat is simple to fix with gelatin, whipped topping and fresh berries. Or try
it with peaches or mandarin oranges and coordinating gelatin flavors.

- 1 package (3 ounces) black cherry *or* cherry gelatin
- 1 cup boiling water
- 1 cup cold water
- 1-1/2 cups fresh blackberries
- 1 carton (8 ounces) frozen whipped topping, thawed
- 1 graham cracker crust (8 to 10 inches)

In a bowl, dissolve gelatin in boiling water. Stir in cold water. Refrigerate for 1 hour or until thickened. Gently fold in blackberries and whipped topping. Pour into crust. Chill for 2 hours or until serving. **Yield:** 8 servings.

Banana Cream Cheese Pie

Zahra Sulemanji, Houston, Texas

(Pictured above and on p. 62)

Whenever I make this creamy banana pie topped with a thick strawberry sauce, everyone looks forward to dessert. The crowd-pleasing recipe was passed on to me by my mother-in-law.

FILLING:
- 1 package (8 ounces) cream cheese, softened
- 1/2 cup sugar
- 1 cup mashed ripe bananas (2 to 3 medium)
- 1 teaspoon lemon juice
- 1 carton (8 ounces) frozen whipped topping, thawed

Cool Refrigerator Pies

1 graham cracker crust (9 inches)
STRAWBERRY TOPPING:
   2 tablespoons sugar
   1 teaspoon cornstarch
1-1/4 cups sliced fresh strawberries
   5 drops red food coloring, optional

In a bowl, beat cream cheese and sugar until smooth. Combine bananas and lemon juice; add to cream cheese mixture. Fold in whipped topping. Pour into crust. Cover and refrigerate for 1 hour or until set. Meanwhile, for strawberry topping, in a saucepan, combine sugar and cornstarch. Stir in strawberries and food coloring if desired. Let stand for 5 minutes. Bring to a boil. Reduce heat; cook and stir for 2 minutes or until thickened. Cool. Drizzle some of the topping over the pie. Cut into slices; serve with the remaining strawberry topping. **Yield:** 6-8 servings.

Fluffy Cranberry Cheese Pie

Mary Parkonen, West Wareham, Massachusetts

(Pictured below)

This pie has a light texture and zippy flavor that matches its vibrant color. It's especially festive for the holidays or anytime of year. And it's easy on the hostess because you can make it ahead.

CRANBERRY TOPPING:
   1 package (3 ounces) raspberry gelatin
   1/3 cup sugar
1-1/4 cups cranberry juice
   1 can (8 ounces) jellied cranberry sauce
FILLING:
   1 package (3 ounces) cream cheese, softened
   1/4 cup sugar
   1 tablespoon milk

   1 teaspoon vanilla extract
1/2 cup whipped topping
   1 pastry shell (9 inches), baked

In a mixing bowl, combine gelatin and sugar; set aside. In a saucepan, bring cranberry juice to a boil. Remove from the heat and pour over gelatin mixture, stirring until dissolved. Stir in the cranberry sauce. Chill until slightly thickened. Meanwhile, in another mixing bowl, beat cream cheese, sugar, milk and vanilla until fluffy. Fold in the whipped topping. Spread evenly into pastry shell. Beat cranberry topping until frothy; spoon over filling. Chill overnight. **Yield:** 6-8 servings.

Pineapple Lime Pie

Mrs. Herbert Fischer, Melbourne, Florida

(Pictured above)

This pie is easy to make and good for any occasion. My husband served in the military for many years and, as we traveled, I served this pie many times.

   1 can (14 ounces) sweetened condensed milk
1/2 cup lime juice
   1 can (8 ounces) crushed pineapple, drained
   2 to 3 drops green food coloring, optional
   1 pastry shell (9 inches), baked *or* 1 graham cracker crust (9 inches)
   1 cup whipping cream
   2 tablespoons sugar
Shaved semisweet chocolate, optional

In a bowl, combine milk, lime juice and pineapple. Stir in food coloring if desired. Spoon into crust. In a small mixing bowl, beat whipping cream until soft peaks form. Beat in the sugar, 1 tablespoon at a time, until stiff peaks form. Spoon over filling. Sprinkle with shaved chocolate if desired. Chill for at least 8 hours or overnight. **Yield:** 6-8 servings.

Peanut Butter 'n' Jelly Pie

Vikki Rebholz, West Chester, Ohio

(Pictured below)

This twist on a traditional twosome will appeal to the young and the young at heart. A chocolate crust holds a peanut butter layer topped with strawberry preserves.

- **1 package (8 ounces) cream cheese, softened**
- **1/2 cup confectioners' sugar**
- **1/3 cup peanut butter**
- **1 chocolate crumb crust (9 inches)**
- **1/2 cup strawberry preserves**
- **2 cups whipped topping**
Additional strawberry preserves, optional

In a mixing bowl, beat cream cheese, sugar and peanut butter until smooth. Spread into crust. Top with preserves and whipped topping. Cover and refrigerate for 4 hours or overnight. If desired, dollop additional preserves on top before serving. **Yield:** 8 servings.

Eggnog Pie

Florence Shaw, East Wenatchee, Washington

A holiday favorite of mine, this creamy pie delivers wonderful eggnog flavor. It's very pretty, too, with a sprinkling of nutmeg on top.

- **1 tablespoon unflavored gelatin**
- **1/4 cup cold water**
- **1/3 cup sugar**
- **2 tablespoons cornstarch**
- **1/4 teaspoon salt**
- **2 cups eggnog***
- **1 teaspoon vanilla extract**
- **1 teaspoon rum extract**
- **1 cup whipping cream, whipped**
- **1 pastry shell (9 inches), baked**

In a small bowl, sprinkle gelatin over water; let stand 1 minute. In a saucepan, combine sugar, cornstarch and salt. Stir in eggnog until smooth. Bring to a boil; cook and stir for 2 minutes or until thickened. Stir in gelatin until dissolved. Remove from the heat; cool to room temperature. Stir in extracts; fold in whipped cream. Pour into pastry shell. Refrigerate until firm. **Yield:** 6-8 servings. **Editor's Note:** This recipe was tested with commercially prepared eggnog.

Ricotta Nut Pie

Renee Bennett, Manlius, New York

I'm proud to serve this tall pie at special dinners for family and guests. Similar to a traditional Italian ricotta pie but with a few fun twists, it's a satisfying dessert that's not overly sweet. No one can resist the yummy combination of almonds, ricotta cheese, apricots and chocolate.

- **1-1/2 cups crushed vanilla wafers (about 45 wafers)**
- **1/4 cup butter *or* margarine, softened**
- **1/3 cup apricot preserves**
- **1 carton (15 ounces) ricotta cheese**
- **1/2 cup sugar**

In a heavy saucepan, bring water to a boil; stir in coffee until dissolved. Reduce heat; add marshmallows and butter. Cook and stir over low heat until marshmallows are melted and mixture is smooth. Set saucepan in ice and whisk mixture constantly until cooled. Fold in whipped cream; spoon into pastry shell. Sprinkle with nuts. Refrigerate for at least 3 hours before serving. Garnish with whipped cream and chocolate curls if desired. **Yield:** 6-8 servings.

Chocolate Truffle Pie

Keri Scofield Lawson, Fullerton, California

(Pictured at left)

I discovered a fast recipe for a delectable chocolate mousse some years ago and thought it might make a good filling for a pie. The chocoholics in our family endorse this scrumptious dessert, saying that it "melts in your mouth"!

> 2 cups (12 ounces) semisweet chocolate chips
> 1-1/2 cups whipping cream, *divided*
> 1/4 cup confectioners' sugar
> 1 tablespoon vanilla extract
> 1 chocolate cookie crust (8 *or* 9 inches)
> Whipped cream and chocolate-covered
>   peppermint candies, optional

In a microwave-safe dish, combine the chocolate chips and 1/2 cup whipping cream; cook, uncovered, on high for 1-2 minutes, stirring every 30 seconds until smooth. Cool to room temperature. Stir in sugar and vanilla; set aside. In a small mixing bowl, beat remaining whipping cream until soft peaks form. Beat in chocolate mixture on high speed, one-third at a time; mix well. Spoon into chocolate cookie crust. Refrigerate for at least 3 hours before serving. Garnish with whipped cream and peppermint candies if desired. **Yield:** 8-10 servings. **Editor's Note:** This recipe was tested in an 850-watt microwave.

> 1 teaspoon vanilla extract
> 3 squares (1 ounce *each*) semisweet
>   chocolate, chopped
> 1/2 cup finely chopped toasted almonds
> 1/4 cup chopped dried apricots
> 1 cup whipping cream, whipped
> 1/4 cup slivered almonds, toasted

Combine the crushed vanilla wafer crumbs and butter; press onto the bottom and up the sides of an ungreased 9-in. pie plate. Bake at 375° for 6-8 minutes or until the crust is lightly browned; cool on a wire rack. Spread apricot preserves over the crust. In a mixing bowl, beat ricotta cheese, sugar and vanilla until smooth. Stir in chocolate, chopped almonds and dried apricots. Fold in whipped cream. Spoon into the crust. Sprinkle with slivered almonds. Cover and refrigerate overnight. **Yield:** 6-8 servings.

Coffee Mallow Pie

Dorothy Smith, El Dorado, Arkansas

(Pictured at right)

This terrific-tasting pie holds up well in the refrigerator overnight to serve family and friends the next day. Coffee lovers will eat up this light and creamy pie, never guessing how easy it was to make.

> 1 cup water
> 1 tablespoon instant coffee granules
> 4 cups miniature marshmallows
> 1 tablespoon butter *or* margarine
> 1 cup whipping cream, whipped
> 1 pastry shell (9 inches), baked
> 1/2 cup chopped walnuts *or* pecans, toasted
> Additional whipped cream and chocolate curls,
>   optional

Fluffy Caramel Pie

Ginger Hendricksen, Wisconsin Rapids, Wisconsin

(Pictured below and on p. 62)

I bake a variety of pies, but this is the one my husband likes best. The gingersnap crumb crust is a tangy contrast to the sweet, lighter-than-air caramel filling. It's the perfect way to end a meal.

1-1/2 cups crushed gingersnaps (about 30 cookies)
1/4 cup butter *or* margarine, melted
FILLING:
1/4 cup cold water
1 envelope unflavored gelatin
28 caramels*
1 cup milk
Dash salt
1/2 cup chopped pecans
1 teaspoon vanilla extract
1 cup whipping cream, whipped
Caramel ice cream topping and additional pecans, optional

Combine the cookie crumbs and butter; press onto the bottom and up the sides of a greased 9-in. pie plate. Cover and chill. Meanwhile, place cold water in a heavy saucepan; sprinkle with gelatin. Let stand for 1 minute. Add caramels, milk and salt; cook and stir over low heat until gelatin is dissolved and caramels are melted. Refrigerate for 1-2 hours or until mixture mounds when stirred with a spoon. Stir in pecans and vanilla. Fold in whipped cream. Pour into crust. Refrigerate for 6 hours or overnight. Garnish with ice cream topping and pecans if desired. Store in the refrigerator. **Yield:** 6-8 servings. ***Editor's Note:** This recipe was tested with Hershey caramels.

Summer Berry Cheese Pie

Mrs. C. Florkewicz, Caldwell, New Jersey

(Pictured above and on p. 62)

I love to make this refreshing pie with fresh blueberries and strawberries from area farms. It's an easy-to-make summer treat that my whole family just gobbles up. I'm sure your family will, too!

1 pint fresh strawberries, sliced, *divided*
1 tablespoon lemon juice
2/3 cup sugar, *divided*
1 package (8 ounces) cream cheese, softened
1 teaspoon grated lemon peel
1 graham cracker crust (9 inches)
2 tablespoons cornstarch
3 to 4 drops red food coloring, optional
1 pint fresh blueberries
Additional grated lemon peel, optional

In a bowl, combine half of the strawberries and lemon juice; mash berries. Add 1/3 cup plus 2 tablespoons sugar; set aside. In a mixing bowl, combine cream cheese, lemon peel and remaining sugar. Spread into the crust. In a saucepan, combine cornstarch and reserved strawberry mixture until blended. Bring to a boil; boil and stir for 2 minutes. Stir in food coloring if desired. Cool slightly. Fold in blueberries and remaining strawberries. Spread over cream cheese mixture. Cover and refrigerate for at least 3 hours. Garnish with additional grated lemon peel if desired. **Yield:** 6-8 servings.

Creamy Peach Pie

Eva Thiessen, Cecil Lake, British Columbia

This extra-speedy peach pie won't tie up your time because no baking is required. Simply stir the ingredients together and refrigerate until serving.

1 package (3 ounces) peach gelatin
2/3 cup boiling water
1 cup vanilla ice cream
1 carton (8 ounces) frozen whipped
   topping, thawed
1 cup diced peeled fresh peaches
1 deep-dish pastry shell (9 inches), baked
Sliced peaches *and/or* mint leaves, optional

In a large bowl, dissolve gelatin in boiling water; stir in ice cream until melted and smooth. Fold in whipped topping. Fold in peaches. Pour into pastry shell. Chill until firm, about 3 hours. Garnish with peaches and/or mint leaves if desired. **Yield:** 6-8 servings.

Cherry Almond Mousse Pie

Dorothy Pritchett, Wills Point, Texas

(Pictured below)

Christmas is the perfect time to treat your family and guests to a festive looking luscious pie featuring chocolate, cherries and nuts in a creamy vanilla mousse. It's a sweet yet light dessert that's the perfect ending to a holiday meal.

1 can (14 ounces) sweetened condensed
   milk, *divided*
1 square (1 ounce) unsweetened chocolate
1/2 teaspoon almond extract, *divided*
1 pastry shell (9 inches), baked
1 jar (10 ounces) maraschino cherries,
   drained
1 package (8 ounces) cream cheese, softened
1 cup cold water
1 package (3.4 ounces) instant vanilla
   pudding mix

1 cup whipping cream, whipped
1/2 cup chopped almonds, toasted
Chocolate curls, optional

In a saucepan over low heat, cook and stir 1/2 cup condensed milk and chocolate until the chocolate is melted and mixture is thickened, about 4 minutes. Stir in 1/4 teaspoon extract. Pour into pastry shell; set aside. Reserve eight whole cherries for garnish. Chop the remaining cherries; set aside. In a mixing bowl, beat the cream cheese until light and fluffy. Gradually beat in the water and remaining milk. Add pudding mix and remaining extract; mix well. Fold in whipped cream, chopped cherries and almonds. Pour over the pie. Chill for 4 hours or until set. Garnish with whole cherries and chocolate curls if desired. **Yield:** 8-10 servings.

Raspberry Ribbon Pie

Victoria Newman, Antelope, California

While he was growing up, this was my husband's favorite Christmas dessert. When we married, his mother passed it on to me. I take it to family gatherings during the holidays and yet to have any to bring home! It's a cool recipe for summer as well.

2 packages (3 ounces *each*) cream cheese,
   softened
1/2 cup confectioners' sugar
Dash salt
1 cup whipping cream, whipped
1 pastry shell with high fluted edge
   (9 inches), baked
1 package (3 ounces) raspberry gelatin
1-1/4 cups boiling water
1 tablespoon lemon juice
1 package (10 ounces) frozen sweetened
   raspberries, thawed

In a mixing bowl, beat the cream cheese, sugar and salt until light and fluffy. Fold in cream. Spread half into pastry shell. Chill for 30 minutes. Meanwhile, dissolve gelatin in water; add lemon juice and raspberries. Carefully spoon half over cream cheese layer; chill until set, about 30 minutes. Let remaining gelatin mixture stand at room temperature. Carefully spread remaining cream cheese mixture over top of pie. Chill for 30 minutes. Top with the remaining gelatin. Chill until firm. **Yield:** 6-8 servings.

Placement of Garnishes

When decorating the top of a pie, plan ahead and place all of the garnishes (cherries, chocolate curls, etc.) between where the pie will be sliced. That way, you won't have to cut through or remove a garnish in order to serve the pie.

White Chocolate Berry Pie

Connie Laux, Englewood, Ohio

(Pictured below and on p. 62)

When strawberries are in season, I love to make this delectable pie. There are fresh berries in each and every luscious bite.

    5 **squares (1 ounce** *each***) white baking chocolate,** *divided*
    2 **tablespoons milk**
    1 **package (3 ounces) cream cheese, softened**
1/3 **cup confectioners' sugar**
    1 **teaspoon grated orange peel**
    1 **cup whipping cream, whipped**
    1 **graham cracker crust (9 inches)**
    2 **cups sliced fresh strawberries**

In a microwave, melt four squares of chocolate with milk. Cool to room temperature. Meanwhile, beat cream cheese and sugar in a small mixing bowl until smooth. Beat in orange peel and melted chocolate. Fold in whipped cream. Spread into crust. Arrange strawberries over top. Melt remaining chocolate; drizzle over berries. Refrigerate for at least 1 hour. Store in the refrigerator. **Yield:** 8 servings.

Fluffy Pineapple Pie

Ozela Haynes, Emerson, Arkansas

Refreshing crushed pineapple adds tropical flair to this fluffy dessert. It is very light, and it isn't overly sweet. Plus, it's easy to make with just a few ingredients I usually have on hand in the refrigerator and pantry. This pretty pie is the perfect ending to any meal.

    2 **cans (8 ounces** *each***) crushed pineapple**
 24 **large marshmallows**
    2 **cups whipped topping**
    1 **graham cracker crust (9 inches)**
Maraschino cherries, optional

Drain pineapple, reserving 1/2 cup juice (discard remaining juice or save for another use). Set the pineapple aside. In a large microwave-safe bowl, combine the juice and marshmallows. Microwave, uncovered, on high for 1 minute; stir. Microwave 1 minute longer; stir until mixture is smooth. Refrigerate for 30 minutes or until slightly thickened and cooled, stirring occasionally. Fold in whipped topping and pineapple. Pour into the graham cracker crust. Cover and refrigerate for 2 hours or until firm. Garnish with cherries if desired. **Yield:** 6-8 servings. **Editor's Note:** This recipe was tested in a 700-watt microwave.

1 carton (8 ounces) frozen whipped
   topping, thawed
1 graham cracker crust (9 inches)

In a bowl, combine gelatin powder and yogurt. Fold in whipped topping. Spread into crust. Refrigerate for at least 20 minutes before serving. **Yield:** 6-8 servings.

Chocolate Mousse Pumpkin Pie

Kathy Peters, Omaha, Nebraska

(Pictured below)

Combine canned pumpkin with two kinds of chocolate in this fluffy autumn delight and you have the perfect pie for special occasions.

   1 cup cooked *or* canned pumpkin
   2 cups miniature marshmallows
1/2 cup milk chocolate chips
1/2 cup miniature semisweet chocolate chips
   1 carton (12 ounces) frozen whipped
     topping, thawed
   1 graham cracker crust (9 inches)
Additional miniature semisweet chocolate
  chips, optional

In a large microwave-safe bowl, combine the pumpkin, marshmallows and chips. Microwave, uncovered, on high for 1-1/2 minutes; stir. Microwave 30-45 seconds longer or until marshmallows are melted and mixture is smooth, stirring every 15 seconds. Cool to room temperature, stirring several times. Set aside about 1 tablespoon of whipped topping. Fold remaining topping into pumpkin mixture. Spoon into crust. Garnish with the reserved topping and miniature chips if desired. Refrigerate for at least 2 hours before serving. **Yield:** 6-8 servings. **Editor's Note:** This recipe was tested in an 850-watt microwave.

Creamy Raspberry Pie

Lorna Nault, Chesterton, Indiana

(Pictured above)

The only thing difficult about this pie is letting it chill. We can't wait for that first light, fluffy slice! It's especially pleasant during warm weather. Depending on what's in season, I might substitute blueberries or strawberries and complementary gelatin flavors.

   1 package (3 ounces) raspberry gelatin
1/2 cup boiling water
   1 cup frozen vanilla yogurt
   1 cup fresh *or* frozen unsweetened
     raspberries
1/4 cup lime juice
   2 cups whipped topping
   1 graham cracker crust (9 inches)
Lime slices and additional raspberries and
  whipped topping, optional

In a bowl, dissolve gelatin in boiling water. Stir in frozen yogurt until melted. Add the raspberries and lime juice. Fold in whipped topping. Spoon into crust. Refrigerate for 3 hours or until firm. Garnish with lime slices, additional raspberries and whipped topping if desired. **Yield:** 8 servings.

Lime Yogurt Pie

Rhonda Olivieri, East Earl, Pennsylvania

If you're running short on time, this pie is a breeze to make because it takes advantage of a prepared graham cracker crust. You can get on with preparing the rest of the meal while this easy-to-make dessert chills in the refrigerator.

   1 package (3 ounces) lime gelatin
   2 cartons (6 ounces *each*) key lime pie
     yogurt

Baking a Pastry Shell

Prick the bottom of the pastry with a fork to prevent it from bubbling while baking. Line the shell with heavy-duty foil and bake at 450° for 8 minutes. Remove the foil and bake 5-6 minutes more or until golden brown. Cool on a wire rack.

Chocolate Mousse Pie

Lois Mulkey, Sublimity, Oregon

(Pictured below)

Sky-high and scrumptious, this fluffy chocolate delight is super to serve to company. You can put the pie together in a wink—and it'll disappear just as fast! For a nice option, mound the filling in a purchased chocolate crumb crust.

- 1 milk chocolate candy bar with almonds (7 ounces)
- 16 large marshmallows *or* 1-1/2 cups miniature marshmallows
- 1/2 cup milk
- 2 cups whipping cream, whipped
- 1 pastry shell, baked *or* graham cracker *or* chocolate crumb crust (8 *or* 9 inches)

Place the candy bar, marshmallows and milk in a heavy saucepan; cook over low heat, stirring constantly until chocolate is melted and mixture is smooth. Cool. Fold in

whipped cream; pour into crust. Refrigerate for at least 3 hours. **Yield:** 6-8 servings.

Peanut Butter Cream Pie

Jesse and Anne Foust, Bluefield, West Virginia

(Pictured above)

During the warm months, it's nice to have a fluffy, no-bake dessert that's a snap to make. Packed with peanut flavor, this pie gets gobbled up even after a big meal! If you have chocolate lovers in your family, use a chocolate crumb crust instead of the graham cracker crust.

- 1 package (8 ounces) cream cheese, softened
- 3/4 cup confectioners' sugar
- 1/2 cup creamy peanut butter
- 6 tablespoons milk
- 1 carton (8 ounces) frozen whipped topping, thawed
- 1 graham cracker crust (9 inches)
- 1/4 cup chopped peanuts

In a large mixing bowl, beat cream cheese until fluffy. Add sugar and peanut butter; mix well. Gradually add the milk; beat until blended. Fold in whipped topping; spoon into the crust. Sprinkle with peanuts. Refrigerate for 8 hours or overnight. **Yield:** 6-8 servings.

Cool Lime Pie

Waydella Hart, Parsons, Kansas

This delightfully sweet-tart pie is pretty to set on the table and so quick and easy to make. It's a sensational warm-weather dessert. But my family requests it throughout the year, too.

- 1 package (8 ounces) cream cheese, softened
- 1 can (14 ounces) sweetened condensed milk
- 3/4 cup limeade concentrate
- 4 drops green food coloring, optional
- 1 carton (8 ounces) frozen whipped topping, thawed, *divided*
- 1 graham cracker crust (9 inches)
- 1 kiwifruit, peeled and sliced

Mandarin oranges and chopped pistachios, optional

In a mixing bowl, beat cream cheese and milk until smooth. Add limeade and food coloring if desired. Fold in half of the whipped topping. Pour into crust. Cover and refrigerate for 2 hours. Top with remaining whipped topping; garnish with kiwi, oranges and pistachios if desired. **Yield:** 6-8 servings.

Refrigerator Orange Pie

Anita Curtis, Camarillo, California

(Pictured below)

For a quick and easy dessert that's cool and refreshing, give this fruity pie a try. It's perfect for summertime. It's also handy since you make it ahead and let it chill in the refrigerator.

- 1 package (8 ounces) cream cheese, softened
- 1 can (14 ounces) sweetened condensed milk

- 1 can (6 ounces) frozen orange juice concentrate, thawed
- 1/2 teaspoon grated orange peel
- 1 graham cracker crust (9 inches)

Orange segments, optional

In a mixing bowl, beat cream cheese until fluffy. Gradually add milk, orange juice concentrate and orange peel. Pour into crust. Refrigerate for at least 12 hours. Garnish with oranges if desired. **Yield:** 6-8 servings.

Pecan Cream Cheese Pie

Mildred Troupe, Wartrace, Tennessee

Toasted coconut, chopped pecans and caramel sauce top a cream cheese layer in this special pie. A friend who loves to give out recipes shared this one with me...I'm so glad she did!

- 1 cup chopped pecans
- 1/2 cup flaked coconut
- 1/4 cup butter *or* margarine, melted
- 4 ounces cream cheese, softened
- 1/4 cup confectioners' sugar
- 1-3/4 cups whipped topping
- 1 pastry shell (9 inches), baked and cooled
- 1/2 cup caramel ice cream topping

In a bowl, combine pecans, coconut and butter. Pour into an ungreased 15-in. x 10-in. x 1-in. baking pan. Bake at 350° for 5-10 minutes or until golden brown, stirring occasionally. Cool. In a mixing bowl, beat the cream cheese and sugar until smooth. Fold in whipped topping. Spoon into pastry shell. Sprinkle with coconut mixture. Drizzle with caramel topping. Refrigerate for 2 hours. **Yield:** 6-8 servings.

p. 86

p. 80

p. 84

p. 81

p. 86

Freezer & Ice Cream Pies

COOL TREATS. Clockwise from upper left: Mint Chocolate Chip Pie (p. 86), Frozen Hawaiian Pie (p. 84), Meringue Berry Pie (p. 80), Frozen Mud Pie (p. 81) and Frosty Lemon Pie (p. 86).

Frozen Pumpkin Pie

Diane Hixon, Niceville, Florida

As a rule, I don't like pumpkin, but this light, melt-in-your-mouth pie is an exception! Just fill a convenient graham cracker crust with a cool combination of canned pumpkin and vanilla ice cream for an unexpected taste sensation.

       3 cups vanilla ice cream, softened
       1 cup cooked *or* canned pumpkin
   1/2 cup packed brown sugar
   1/4 teaspoon salt
   1/4 teaspoon *each* ground cinnamon, ginger
          and nutmeg
       1 graham cracker crust (9 inches)

In a mixing bowl, combine ice cream, pumpkin, brown sugar, salt, cinnamon, ginger and nutmeg; mix well. Pour into crust. Freeze for 4 hours or until firm. Remove from the freezer 5-10 minutes before serving. **Yield:** 6-8 servings.

Milk Chocolate Pie

Kathy Crow, Payson, Arizona

(Pictured below)

This is the best chocolate pie I've ever had, and, believe me, I've tried a lot of chocolaty creations over the years! It's cool, rich and melts in your mouth. Best of all, it takes just 10 minutes to whip up and pop in the freezer. Keep this prepared pie on hand for last-minute entertaining.

       1 cup milk chocolate chips
   1/2 cup milk, *divided*

       1 package (3 ounces) cream cheese,
          softened
       1 carton (8 ounces) frozen whipped
          topping, thawed
       1 chocolate crumb crust (9 inches)
**Milk chocolate kisses and additional whipped
   topping, optional**

In a microwave or heavy saucepan, combine chocolate chips and 1/4 cup milk. Cook until chips are melted; stir until smooth. In a mixing bowl, beat the cream cheese and remaining milk until smooth. Gradually beat in the melted chocolate mixture. Fold in whipped topping. Pour into the chocolate crumb crust. Freeze for 4-6 hours or overnight. May be frozen for up to 3 months. Remove from the freezer 5-10 minutes before serving. Garnish with chocolate kisses and whipped topping if desired. **Yield:** 6-8 servings.

Frozen Raspberry Pie

Dorothy Latta-McCarty, Lakewood, Colorado

Guests' eyes will light up at the sight of this appealing make-ahead pie. The light raspberry flavor is accented by the pleasant crunch of toasted almonds. It's especially refreshing in summer, but my family and friends enjoy it year-round.

       1 jar (7 ounces) marshmallow creme
       1 cup (8 ounces) raspberry yogurt
       1 cup raspberry sherbet, softened
       2 cups whipped topping
   1/2 cup chopped slivered almonds, toasted
       1 graham cracker crust (9 inches)
**Additional whipped topping and almonds,
   optional**

Place marshmallow creme in a deep microwave-safe bowl. Microwave, uncovered, on high for 1 minute or until marshmallow creme puffs; stir until smooth. Cool to room temperature, stirring several times. Stir in yogurt and sherbet until blended. Fold in whipped topping and toasted almonds. Pour into the graham cracker crust. Cover and freeze for 6 hours or overnight. Remove from the freezer 10-15 minutes before serving. Garnish with whipped topping and almonds if desired. **Yield:** 6-8 servings. **Editor's Note:** This recipe was tested in a 700-watt microwave.

Making Crumb Crusts

When making a from-scratch crumb crust, use your fingers to press the crumbs evenly over the bottom and up the sides of the pie plate. Then press another pie plate of the same size firmly into the crust to make it smooth.

Caramel Pie

Ozela Haynes, Emerson, Arkansas

(Pictured above)

I got the recipe for this sweet, fluffy dessert from my niece. Whenever this pie is served, it goes fast! You'll find yourself making this pleasing pie even when you do have time.

- **4 ounces cream cheese, softened**
- **1/2 cup sweetened condensed milk**
- **1 carton (8 ounces) frozen whipped topping, thawed**
- **1 graham cracker crust (9 inches)**
- **1/2 cup caramel ice cream topping**
- **3/4 cup flaked coconut, toasted**
- **1/4 cup chopped pecans, toasted**

In a mixing bowl, blend cream cheese and milk; fold in the whipped topping. Spread half into the crust. Drizzle with half of the caramel topping. Combine coconut and pecans; sprinkle half over the caramel. Repeat layers. Freeze for 4-6 hours or overnight. Remove from the freezer 10-15 minutes before serving. **Yield:** 6-8 servings.

Lemon Cheese Pie

Laura Odell, Eden, North Carolina

(Pictured at right)

This pie can be made ahead and frozen. So it's not unusual for me to have one ready in the freezer to serve to unexpected company.

- **1 package (8 ounces) cream cheese, softened**
- **2 cups cold milk, *divided***
- **1 package (3.4 ounces) instant lemon pudding mix**
- **1/2 teaspoon grated lemon peel**
- **1 graham cracker crust (9 inches)**

In a small mixing bowl, beat cream cheese on low speed until smooth. Gradually add 1/2 cup milk. Sprinkle with pudding mix. Gradually add the remaining milk. Add the lemon peel; beat until thickened, about 5 minutes. Pour into the graham cracker crust. Freeze for 4-6 hours or overnight. Remove from the freezer 5-10 minutes before serving. **Yield:** 6-8 servings.

Cookies 'n' Cream Pie

Julie Sterchi, Flora, Illinois

Convenience foods—including instant pudding, frozen whipped topping, cookies and a prepared crumb crust—make this a treat for the cook, too. Fans of cookies 'n' cream ice cream will fall for this do-ahead dessert.

- **1-1/2 cups cold half-and-half cream**
- **1 package (3.4 ounces) instant vanilla pudding mix**
- **1 carton (8 ounces) frozen whipped topping, thawed**
- **1 cup crushed cream-filled chocolate sandwich cookies (about 11 cookies)**
- **1 chocolate crumb crust (9 inches)**

In a small mixing bowl, combine the cream and pudding mix; beat on low speed for 2 minutes. Let stand for 5 minutes or until thickened. Fold in whipped topping and cookies. Spoon into crust. Freeze until firm, about 6 hours or overnight. May be frozen for up to 3 months. Remove from the freezer 10 minutes before serving. **Yield:** 6-8 servings.

Lazy-Day Grasshopper Pie

Carol Severson, Shelton, Washington

Dazzle dinner guests with this eye-pleasing pie! It's simple to put together the night before, and it's light, cool and refreshing—with just the right amount of mint.

    1 jar (7 ounces) marshmallow creme
1/4 cup milk
    6 to 8 drops peppermint extract
    6 to 8 drops green food coloring
    1 cup whipping cream, whipped
    1 chocolate crumb crust (9 inches)
Shaved chocolate and additional whipped cream, optional

In a mixing bowl, beat marshmallow creme, milk, extract and food coloring until smooth. Fold in whipped cream. Spoon into the crust. Cover and freeze overnight or until firm. Remove from the freezer 20 minutes before serving. Garnish with shaved chocolate and whipped cream if desired. **Yield:** 6-8 servings.

Meringue Berry Pie

Page Alexander, Baldwin City, Kansas

(Pictured above and on p. 76)

A hot day calls for a cool dessert like this taste-tempting pie. Fresh berries and a sweet raspberry sauce over ice cream in a meringue crust make each slice absolutely irresistible.

1/2 cup sugar, *divided*
1/4 cup slivered almonds, toasted and ground
    2 tablespoons cornstarch
    2 egg whites
1/8 teaspoon cream of tartar
SAUCE AND TOPPING:
1/2 cup sugar
    1 tablespoon cornstarch
1/3 cup water
    1 pint fresh *or* frozen raspberries
    1 quart vanilla ice cream
    2 cups fresh mixed berries

In a small bowl, combine 1/4 cup sugar, almonds and cornstarch; mix well. In a small mixing bowl, beat egg whites at high speed until foamy. Add cream of tartar; continue beating until soft peaks form. Gradually add remaining sugar; beat until stiff peaks form. Fold in almond mixture. Spread over the bottom and up the sides of a greased 9-in. pie plate. Bake at 275° for 1 to 1-1/2 hours or until light golden brown. Turn off oven; do not open door. Let cool in oven for 1 hour. Remove from the oven and cool completely. Meanwhile, for sauce, combine sugar and cornstarch in a saucepan. Gradually stir in water until smooth. Add raspberries; bring to a boil over medium heat, stirring constantly. Boil for 1 minute or until thickened; set aside. Cool. To serve, scoop ice cream onto meringue; top with mixed berries and sauce. Serve immediately. Store leftovers in the freezer. **Yield:** 6-8 servings.

Peach Melba Ice Cream Pie

Judy Vaske, Bancroft, Iowa

(Pictured below)

On a hot summer night, this cool pie makes a very refreshing dessert. Like most wonderful recipes, it came from a very dear friend.

1-1/2 cups flaked coconut
1/3 cup chopped pecans
    3 tablespoons butter *or* margarine, melted
    1 quart frozen peach yogurt, softened
    1 pint vanilla ice cream, softened
    1 tablespoon cornstarch

1 tablespoon sugar
1 package (10 ounces) frozen sweetened
  raspberries, thawed
1 cup sliced fresh *or* frozen peaches, thawed

Combine coconut, pecans and butter; press onto the bottom and up the sides of an ungreased 9-in. pie plate. Bake at 350° for 12 minutes or until crust begins to brown around edges. Cool completely. Spoon frozen yogurt into crust; smooth the top. Spread ice cream over yogurt. Cover and freeze for 2 hours or until firm. In a small saucepan, combine cornstarch and sugar. Drain raspberry juice into pan; stir until smooth. Bring to a boil; cook and stir for 2 minutes or until thickened. Remove from the heat; add raspberries. Cover and refrigerate. Remove pie from freezer 10 minutes before serving. Arrange peaches over top of pie; drizzle with some of the sauce. Serve the remaining sauce. **Yield:** 6-8 servings.

Strawberry Rhubarb Ice Cream Pie

Connie Fleck, Fort Atkinson, Wisconsin

This extra-speedy ice cream pie will keep your stay in the kitchen short but with scrumptious results. It combines two of my favorite fresh fruits—rhubarb and strawberries.

1 quart vanilla ice cream, softened
1 graham cracker crust (9 inches)
1-1/2 cups sliced fresh *or* frozen rhubarb
  (1/2-inch pieces)
1/2 cup sugar
1 tablespoon cornstarch
1 tablespoon water
1 pint fresh strawberries, sliced

Spoon ice cream into crust; freeze. Meanwhile, in a saucepan over medium heat, cook rhubarb and sugar, stirring occasionally, until sugar is dissolved and mixture comes to a boil. Combine cornstarch and water; stir into saucepan. Cook and stir for 2 minutes or until thickened. Cool. Fold in berries; refrigerate. Spread over ice cream. Freeze for 4-6 hours or overnight. Remove from the freezer 10 minutes before serving. **Yield:** 8 servings.

Freezer Peanut Butter Pie

Nina Rufener, Mansfield, Ohio

If you like peanut butter, you're going to love this pie! It can be made ahead and frozen, so it's perfect for drop-in guests.

1 quart vanilla ice cream, softened, *divided*
1 graham cracker crust (8 *or* 9 inches)
1/2 cup peanut butter
1/3 cup light corn syrup
Chocolate sauce
Chopped walnuts

Spread half of the ice cream into the graham cracker crust. Combine peanut butter and corn syrup until blend-

ed; spread over ice cream. Spread the remaining ice cream evenly over the top. Drizzle with chocolate sauce; sprinkle with nuts. Cover and freeze for 3-4 hours or until firm. Remove from freezer 15 minutes before serving. **Yield:** 6-8 servings.

Frozen Mud Pie

Debbie Terenzini, Lusby, Maryland

(Pictured above and on p. 76)

Here's one of those "looks like you fussed" desserts that is so easy it's become a standard for me. I love the mocha version, but pure chocolate lovers may prefer using chocolate chip ice cream. The cookie crust is a snap to make.

1-1/2 cups crushed cream-filled chocolate
  sandwich cookies (about 15 cookies)
1-1/2 teaspoons sugar, optional
1/4 cup butter *or* margarine, melted
2 pints chocolate chip *or* coffee ice cream,
  softened
1/4 cup chocolate syrup, *divided*
Additional cream-filled chocolate sandwich
  cookies, optional

In a bowl, combine cookie crumbs and sugar if desired. Stir in butter. Press onto the bottom and up the sides of an ungreased 9-in. pie plate. Refrigerate for 30 minutes. Spoon 1 pint of ice cream into crust. Drizzle with half of the chocolate syrup; cut through ice cream with a knife to swirl the chocolate sauce. Carefully top with remaining ice cream. Drizzle with remaining syrup; swirl with a knife. Cover and freeze until firm. Remove from the freezer 10-15 minutes before serving. Garnish with whole cookies if desired. **Yield:** 8 servings.

Black-Bottom Ice Cream Pie

Mrs. Malvin Mauney Jr., Cordova, Tennessee
(Pictured below)

Since we live in an area where dairy farming flourishes, an ice cream pie seemed like a natural dish for me to create. It's an easy dessert to prepare anytime. I've made it often over the years, and I've never met a person who didn't enjoy a big slice.

1-1/2 cups crushed gingersnaps (about 24
    cookies)
1/4 cup confectioners' sugar
1/3 cup butter *or* margarine, melted
  1 cup chocolate ice cream, softened
  1 cup (6 ounces) semisweet chocolate chips
1/2 cup whipping cream
1/2 teaspoon vanilla extract
  1 quart vanilla ice cream, softened

In a bowl, combine cookie crumbs, sugar and butter. Press onto the bottom and up the sides of an ungreased 9-in. pie plate. Refrigerate for at least 30 minutes. Spoon chocolate ice cream into crust; freeze until firm, about 1 hour. Meanwhile, in a heavy saucepan, melt chocolate chips with cream over low heat, stirring constantly. Remove from the heat; add vanilla. Cool. Spread half of the chocolate sauce over chocolate ice cream; freeze until set, about 1 hour. Spoon vanilla ice cream over chocolate sauce; freeze until firm, about 1 hour. Spread remaining chocolate sauce evenly over pie; freeze for 4-6 hours or overnight. Remove from the freezer 5-10 minutes before serving. **Yield:** 6-8 servings. **Editor's Note:** This dessert takes time to make since each layer must be set before the next layer is added.

Spectacular Ice Cream Pie

Gladys McCollum Abee, McKee, Kentucky

Biting into this melt-in-your-mouth treat is like having coffee and dessert together. To avoid the holiday baking crunch, you can make it ahead of time and store it in the freezer until you are ready to serve.

  1 cup graham cracker crumbs (about 16
    squares)
1/2 cup finely chopped walnuts
1/3 cup butter *or* margarine, melted
  1 pint coffee ice cream *or* flavor of your
    choice, softened
  1 pint vanilla ice cream, softened
SAUCE:
  3 tablespoons butter *or* margarine
  1 cup packed brown sugar
1/2 cup half-and-half cream
  1 cup finely chopped walnuts
  1 teaspoon vanilla extract

In a small bowl, combine the graham cracker crumbs, walnuts and butter; press onto the bottom and up the sides of a greased 9-in. pie plate. Bake at 375° for 8-10 minutes. Remove to a wire rack to cool completely. Spread coffee ice cream over crust. Freeze for 2 hours or until firm. Repeat with vanilla ice cream. Remove pie from the freezer 15 minutes before serving. For the sauce, combine butter and brown sugar in a small saucepan; cook and stir over low heat for 5-6 minutes. Remove from the heat; slowly stir in half-and-half cream. Cook and stir 1 minute longer. Remove from the heat; stir in walnuts and vanilla. Serve warm over slices of pie. **Yield:** 8-10 servings.

Chocolate Sundae Pie

Barbara Soyars, Danville, Virginia

I keep one of these cool and creamy chocolate desserts in my freezer at all times. I've taken it to potluck dinners, church suppers and family get-togethers, and it's always well received.

  4 ounces cream cheese, softened
1/2 cup sweetened condensed milk
  4 teaspoons baking cocoa
  1 carton (8 ounces) frozen whipped topping,
    thawed
  1 chocolate crumb crust (9 inches)
1/2 cup chocolate syrup
1/2 cup chopped pecans

In a small mixing bowl, beat cream cheese until smooth. Beat in the sweetened condensed milk and baking cocoa until smooth. Fold in whipped topping. Spoon into chocolate crumb crust. Drizzle with chocolate syrup and chopped pecans. Cover and freeze overnight. Remove from the freezer 5-10 minutes before serving. **Yield:** 6-8 servings.

1 can (12 ounces) evaporated milk
36 vanilla wafers
1 cup sugar
1 envelope (.14 ounce) unsweetened
    lemon-lime Kool-Aid
Whipped topping, optional

Pour milk into a small metal or glass mixing bowl. Add mixer beaters to the bowl. Cover and chill for at least 2 hours. Coat a 9-in. pie plate with nonstick cooking spray. Line bottom and sides of plate with wafers. Beat milk until soft peaks form. Add sugar and drink mix; beat until thoroughly mixed. Spoon over wafers; cover and freeze for at least 4 hours. Remove from the freezer 5-10 minutes before serving. Garnish with whipped topping if desired. **Yield:** 6-8 servings.

Strawberry-Topped Yogurt Pie

Nancy Gordon, Kansas City, Missouri

(Pictured below)

This tangy make-ahead pie has been one of our family's favorite desserts for more than 15 years. You can top it with most any fruit.

1 package (8 ounces) cream cheese,
    softened
2/3 cup plain yogurt
1/3 cup nonfat dry milk powder
1/3 cup honey
1 graham cracker crust (8 inches)
2 cups diced fresh strawberries
Orange peel strips, optional

In a mixing bowl, beat cream cheese, yogurt, milk powder and honey. Spoon into crust. Cover and freeze for up to 1 month. Remove from the freezer 30 minutes before serving. Top with strawberries. Garnish with orange peel if desired. **Yield:** 8 servings.

Scoops of Ice Cream Pie

Beverly Gottfried, Candler, North Carolina

(Pictured above)

My kitchen is a popular spot when I serve up this deluxe dessert on hot summer days. Garnished with raspberries, each slice features smooth vanilla ice cream piled on a nutty chocolate crust. Eliminate last-minute fuss by preparing and freezing this pretty pie ahead of time.

2 pints vanilla ice cream, *divided*
1 cup chocolate wafer crumbs (about 16
    wafers)
1/2 cup chopped almonds
1/4 cup butter *or* margarine, melted
Fresh raspberries
Fresh mint, optional

Soften 1 pint of ice cream. Combine the cookie crumbs, nuts and butter. Press onto the bottom and up the sides of a 9-in. pie plate. Spread with the softened ice cream. Cover and freeze until firm. Scoop remaining ice cream into small balls; pile into crust. Cover and freeze for up to 2 months. Remove from the freezer 10 minutes before serving. Arrange raspberries between scoops. Garnish with mint if desired. **Yield:** 6-8 servings.

Kool-Aid Pie

Ledia Black, Pineland, Texas

A fun crust of vanilla wafers is easy for kids to make and holds an eye-catching fluffy filling that's refreshing in summer. Use different flavors of Kool-Aid to vary the pie's taste.

easy to put together, and everyone always asks for a copy of the recipe.

- 1 package (8 ounces) cream cheese, softened
- 1 cup confectioners' sugar
- 1 can (16 ounces) whole-berry cranberry sauce
- 1 carton (8 ounces) frozen whipped topping, thawed
- 2 pastry shells (9 inches), baked*

Additional whipped topping, optional
Slivered almonds, toasted, optional

In a mixing bowl, beat cream cheese and sugar until smooth. Stir in cranberry sauce. Fold in whipped topping. Spoon into crusts. Cover and freeze for up to 3 months. Remove from the freezer 10-15 minutes before serving. Garnish with whipped topping and almonds if desired. **Yield:** 2 pies (6-8 servings each). ***Editor's Note:** Shortbread or graham cracker crusts may be substituted for the pastry shells.

Chilly Coconut Pie

Jeannette Mack, Rushville, New York

Everyone loves this creamy coconut pie. It's so easy to make that I keep several in the freezer for those occasions when I need a quick dessert.

- 1 package (3 ounces) cream cheese, softened
- 2 tablespoons sugar
- 1/2 cup milk
- 1/4 teaspoon almond extract
- 1 cup flaked coconut
- 1 carton (8 ounces) frozen whipped topping, thawed
- 1 graham cracker crust (9 inches)

In a mixing bowl, beat cream cheese and sugar until smooth. Gradually beat in milk and extract. Fold in coconut and whipped topping. Spoon into crust. Cover and freeze for at least 4 hours. Remove from the freezer 30 minutes before serving. **Yield:** 6-8 servings.

Carrot Ice Cream Pie

Bethel Anderson, St. James, Minnesota

This refreshing dessert tastes a little bit like orange sherbet. My guests are always surprised to learn they're eating carrots. But they all agree the deliciously different pie is rooted in good taste!

- 1-1/3 cups graham cracker crumbs (about 21 squares)
- 1/3 cup packed brown sugar
- 1/3 cup butter *or* margarine, melted
- 1/3 cup lemonade concentrate
- 2-1/4 cups chopped carrots

Frozen Hawaiian Pie

Jennifer McQuillan, Jacksonville, Florida

(Pictured above and on p. 76)

Cool summer pies are one of my mom's specialties. This version offers pineapple, maraschino cherries and walnuts that are folded into a fluffy filling. It's an easy yet tempting no-bake dessert.

- 1 can (14 ounces) sweetened condensed milk
- 1 carton (12 ounces) frozen whipped topping, thawed
- 1 can (20 ounces) crushed pineapple, drained
- 1/2 cup chopped walnuts
- 1/2 cup chopped maraschino cherries
- 2 tablespoons lemon juice
- 2 graham cracker crusts (9 inches)

Fresh mint and additional walnuts and maraschino cherries

In a bowl, combine milk and whipped topping. Gently fold in pineapple, nuts, cherries and lemon juice. Pour into the crusts. Freeze until firm, about 4 hours. Remove from the freezer 20 minutes before serving. Garnish with mint, nuts and cherries. **Yield:** 2 pies (6-8 servings each).

Frosty Cranberry Pie

Mildred Skrha, Oak Brook, Illinois

It's nice to have this light, not-too-sweet pie in the freezer when unexpected guests stop over for coffee. It's so

    1/4 cup sugar
    1 quart vanilla ice cream, softened

In a small bowl, combine cracker crumbs and brown sugar; stir in butter. Press onto the bottom and up the sides of an ungreased 9-in. pie plate. Refrigerate for 30 minutes. Meanwhile, place lemonade concentrate, carrots and sugar in a food processor or blender; cover and process until carrots are finely chopped and mixture is blended. Transfer to a bowl; stir in ice cream until well blended. Pour into crust. Cover and freeze for 8 hours or overnight. Remove from the freezer 15-20 minutes before serving. **Yield:** 6-8 servings.

Pumpkin Ice Cream Pie

Suzanne McKinley, Lyons, Georgia

(Pictured below)

Although it looks like you fussed, this pretty layered pie is easy to assemble with convenient canned pumpkin, store-bought candy bars and a prepared crust.

    3 English toffee candy bars (1.4 ounces *each*),
        crushed, *divided*
    3 cups vanilla ice cream, softened, *divided*
    1 chocolate crumb crust (9 inches)
    1/2 cup canned *or* cooked pumpkin
    2 tablespoons sugar
    1/2 teaspoon ground cinnamon
    1/4 teaspoon ground nutmeg

Combine two-thirds of the crushed candy bars and 2 cups ice cream. Spoon into crust; freeze for 1 hour or until firm. In a bowl, combine the pumpkin, sugar, cinnamon, nutmeg and remaining ice cream. Spoon over

ice cream layer in crust. Sprinkle with remaining crushed candy bars. Cover and freeze for 8 hours or up to 2 months. Remove from the freezer 10-15 minutes before serving. **Yield:** 8 servings.

Sunshine Ice Cream Pie

Bonnie Polson, Moravia, Iowa

(Pictured above)

Many people tell me this pretty and easy-to-make frozen dessert tastes like the Dreamsicles they loved as young children.

    1 pint vanilla ice cream, softened
    1 graham cracker crust (8 *or* 9 inches)
    1 pint orange sherbet, softened
    2 cups whipped topping
    1 can (11 ounces) mandarin oranges,
        drained
    2 tablespoons flaked coconut, toasted

Spread ice cream into the crust; spread sherbet over ice cream. Freeze for at least 3 hours. Top with whipped topping. Cover and freeze. Remove from the freezer 30 minutes before servng. Arrange oranges on top and sprinkle with coconut. **Yield:** 6-8 servings.

Softening Ice Cream

Ice cream can be softened quickly by microwaving it at 30% power for about 30 seconds. Repeat if necessary.

Mint Chocolate Chip Pie

Dolores Scofield, West Shokan, New York

(Pictured on p. 76)

You'll need only three ingredients to fix this refreshing make-ahead dessert that features a cool combination of mint and chocolate. When time is short, it's so handy to pull this no-fuss pie out of the freezer for company.

- **6 to 8 cups mint chocolate chip ice cream, softened**
- **1 chocolate crumb crust (9 inches)**
- **2 squares (1 ounce *each*) semisweet chocolate**

Spoon ice cream into crust. In a microwave-safe bowl, melt chocolate; stir until smooth. Drizzle over ice cream. Freeze for 6-8 hours or overnight. Remove from the freezer 15 minutes before serving. Pie may be frozen for up to 2 months. **Yield:** 6-8 servings.

Frosty Lemon Pie

Judith Wilke, Dousman, Wisconsin

(Pictured below and on p. 76)

This lemon pie is a nice light and refreshing finish to a summer patio supper. If you're expecting company or simply want a convenient on-hand dessert, give this recipe a try.

- **3/4 cup sugar**
- **1/3 cup lemon juice**
- **1/4 cup butter *or* margarine**
- **Dash salt**

- **3 eggs, beaten**
- **2 pints vanilla ice cream, softened, *divided***
- **1 graham cracker crust (9 inches)**
- **Whipped topping, fresh mint and lemon peel, optional**

In a small saucepan, combine the sugar, lemon juice, butter and salt; cook and stir over medium heat until sugar is dissolved and the butter is melted. Add a small amount of hot mixture to the eggs; return all to the pan. Cook and stir over medium heat until thickened (do not boil). Refrigerate until completely cooled. Spread half of the ice cream into the graham cracker crust; freeze for 1 hour or until firm. Cover with half of the lemon mixture; freeze for 1 hour or until firm. Repeat layers. Cover and freeze for several hours or overnight. Remove from the freezer 10 minutes before serving. If desired, garnish with whipped topping, mint and lemon peel. **Yield:** 8 servings.

Frozen Cherry Cream Pie

Kristyn Hall, Mt. Clemens, Michigan

This pretty pink pie is a cool and tangy treat any time of the year. It's convenient to make and freeze ahead of time. To serve, just cut it and top individual slices with whipped cream.

- **4 ounces cream cheese, softened**
- **1-1/2 cups cherry pie filling**
- **2 cups whipped topping**
- **1 graham cracker crust (9 inches)**

In a mixing bowl, beat cream cheese until smooth. Fold in the pie filling and whipped topping until blended. Spoon into crust. Cover and freeze for 8 hours or overnight. Remove from the freezer 15 minutes before serving. **Yield:** 8 servings.

dinner? Try this delicious pie! It's very festive looking, and folks fall for the minty flavor.

4-1/2 cups crisp rice cereal
   1 cup (6 ounces) semisweet chocolate chips, melted
   2 quarts peppermint stick ice cream, softened
Chocolate syrup *or* chocolate fudge topping
Crushed peppermint candies

Combine the cereal and melted chocolate; mix well. Press onto the bottom and up the sides of an ungreased 10-in. pie plate. Freeze for 5 minutes. Spoon ice cream into the crust. Freeze for 6 hours or overnight. Remove from freezer 15 minutes before serving. Garnish with the chocolate syrup and peppermint candies. **Yield:** 6-8 servings.

Frosty Orange Pie

Jo Magic, Worth, Illinois

The night before expecting company, I whip together this rich creamy pie with pleasant orange flavor. It's also refreshing made with lemonade concentrate.

   1 package (8 ounces) cream cheese, softened
   1 can (14 ounces) sweetened condensed milk
   1 can (6 ounces) frozen orange juice concentrate, thawed
   1 carton (8 ounces) frozen whipped topping, thawed
   1 graham cracker crust (9 inches)

In a mixing bowl, beat cream cheese and condensed milk until smooth. Beat in orange juice concentrate. Fold in whipped topping. Spoon into crust. Cover and freeze for up to 3 months. Remove from the freezer 5-10 minutes before serving. **Yield:** 6-8 servings.

Soda Fountain Pie

Marsha Hanson, Ponsford, Minnesota

(Pictured above)

The first time I made this pie was during winter, using frozen berries. It was a hit even then. For a change of pace, I sometimes make this ice cream pie with an Oreo cookie crust.

1-1/2 cups crushed sugar cones (about 12)
   1/2 cup butter *or* margarine, melted
   1/4 cup sugar
3-1/2 cups fresh strawberries, *divided*
   1 quart vanilla ice cream, softened
   1/3 cup malted milk powder
1-1/2 cups fudge ice cream topping, softened
Additional strawberries, optional

Combine crushed sugar cones, butter and sugar. Press onto the bottom and up the sides of an ungreased 10-in. pie plate. Freeze. Place 3 cups of strawberries in a blender or food processor; cover and puree. Chop the remaining strawberries. Place pureed and chopped strawberries in a large bowl. Add ice cream and malted milk powder; stir to blend. Pour into prepared crust. Cover and freeze overnight. Spread fudge topping over the pie to within 1 in. of edge; freeze for at least 2 hours. Remove from the freezer 20 minutes before serving. Garnish with additional berries if desired. **Yield:** 8-10 servings.

Peppermint Stick Pie

Mildred Peachey, Wooster, Ohio

(Pictured at right)

What's a cook to do when days are filled with holiday preparations and you need to fix a dessert in time for

p. 99

p. 94

p. 90

p. 97

p. 96

Crisps & Cobblers

CRUMBLY CREATIONS. Clockwise from upper left: Caramel Apricot Grunt (p. 99), Berry Apple Crumble (p. 94), Fresh Fruit Cobbler (p. 90), Black and Blue Cobbler (p. 96) and Sweet Potato Cobbler (p. 97).

Fresh Fruit Cobbler

Paula Chick, Lewiston, Maine

(Pictured above and on p. 88)

I received this recipe years ago. It's a family favorite, especially when Maine blueberries are in season. What a treat to eat on a hot summer day!

    5 to 6 cups chopped fresh fruit (apples, rhubarb, blueberries *or* peaches)*
    2 cups all-purpose flour
    1/2 cup sugar
    4 teaspoons baking powder
    1 teaspoon salt
    1/2 cup cold butter *or* margarine
    1 cup milk
TOPPING:
    2/3 cup sugar
    1/4 cup cornstarch
    1-1/2 cups boiling water

Arrange fruit evenly in a 13-in. x 9-in. x 2-in. greased baking pan. In a bowl, combine flour, sugar, baking powder and salt; cut in butter until crumbly. Stir in milk just until blended. Spoon over fruit. Combine sugar and cornstarch; sprinkle over batter. Pour boiling water over all. Bake at 350° for 40-45 minutes or until fruit is tender. **Yield:** 12-16 servings. ***Editor's Note:** If desired, a combination of apples and rhubarb or blueberries and peaches can be used.

Cranberry Crumble

Karen Riordan, Louisville, Kentucky

My family likes this crumble so much I make it year-round. But I especially like to serve it warm on cool winter evenings.

1-1/2 cups quick-cooking oats
    1 cup packed brown sugar
    1/2 cup all-purpose flour

    1/3 cup cold butter *or* margarine
    1 can (16 ounces) whole-berry cranberry sauce
Whipped cream *or* ice cream, optional

In a bowl, combine oats, brown sugar and flour. Cut in butter until crumbly. Press half into a greased 8-in. square baking dish. Spread the cranberry sauce evenly over top. Sprinkle with remaining oat mixture. Bake at 350° for 35-40 minutes or until topping is golden brown and filling is bubbly. Serve warm with whipped cream or ice cream if desired. **Yield:** 9 servings.

Blueberry Raspberry Crunch

Harriett Catlin, Nanticoke, Maryland

This quick-to-fix dessert comes in handy when I need to make something sweet in a hurry. I often have the ingredients in my pantry.

    1 can (21 ounces) blueberry pie filling
    1 can (21 ounces) raspberry pie filling
    1 package (18-1/4 ounces) white cake mix
    1/2 cup chopped walnuts
    1/2 cup butter *or* margarine, melted

Combine the blueberry and raspberry pie fillings in a greased 13-in. x 9-in. x 2-in. baking dish. In a bowl, combine the cake mix, walnuts and butter until crumbly; sprinkle over the filling. Bake at 375° for 25-30 minutes or until topping is golden brown and filling is bubbly. Serve warm. **Yield:** 12 servings.

Cinnamon Peach Cobbler

Victoria Lowe, Lititz, Pennsylvania

Prepared biscuit mix makes this comforting cobbler a quick favorite. My husband loves the warm peaches, cinnamony sauce and golden crumb topping.

    4 cups sliced peeled fresh *or* frozen unsweetened peaches, thawed

1/2 cup sugar
1 tablespoon plus 2/3 cup biscuit/baking mix, *divided*
1/2 teaspoon ground cinnamon
2 to 3 tablespoons brown sugar
1/4 cup cold butter *or* margarine
3 tablespoons milk

In a bowl, combine peaches, sugar, 1 tablespoon of biscuit mix and cinnamon. Transfer to a greased shallow 1-1/2-qt. baking dish. In a bowl, combine the brown sugar and remaining biscuit mix. Cut in butter until crumbly. Stir in milk just until blended. Drop by rounded tablespoonfuls onto peach mixture. Bake at 400° for 20-25 minutes or until topping is golden brown and filling is bubbly. **Yield:** 6-8 servings.

Cherry Nut Crisp

Melissa Radulovich, Byers, Colorado

(Pictured below)

I used my favorite cherry pie recipe to create this crisp after my fiance—now my husband—asked me to make a treat for his rugby team. Since I didn't have time to roll out a crust, I just used a simple crisp crust.

2 cans (14-1/2 ounces *each*) pitted tart cherries
1 cup sugar
1/4 cup quick-cooking tapioca
1 teaspoon almond extract
1/8 teaspoon salt
4 to 5 drops red food coloring, optional
CRUST:
1 cup all-purpose flour
1/3 cup sugar
1/4 teaspoon salt
1/8 teaspoon baking powder
6 tablespoons butter *or* margarine, melted

TOPPING:
1/2 cup all-purpose flour
1/2 cup packed brown sugar
1/2 cup chopped pecans
1/3 cup quick-cooking oats
6 tablespoons cold butter *or* margarine

Drain cherries, reserving 3/4 cup juice (discard remaining juice or save for another use). In a bowl, combine the cherries, sugar, tapioca, extract, salt, food coloring if desired and reserved juice; set aside for 15 minutes, stirring occasionally. Meanwhile, combine crust ingredients. Press onto the bottom and 1 in. up the sides of a greased 9-in. square baking dish; set aside. In another bowl, combine the first four topping ingredients; cut in butter until mixture resembles coarse crumbs. Stir the cherry mixture; pour into crust. Sprinkle with topping. Bake at 400° for 10 minutes. Reduce heat to 375°; bake 30-35 minutes longer or until topping is golden brown and filling is bubbly. **Yield:** 9 servings.

Quick Strawberry Cobbler

Sue Poe, Hayden, Alabama

(Pictured above)

Blueberry or cherry pie filling also works great with this easy cobbler. A good friend shared the recipe with me.

2 cans (21 ounces *each*) strawberry pie filling *or* fruit filling of your choice
1/2 cup butter *or* margarine, softened
1 package (3 ounces) cream cheese, softened
2 teaspoons vanilla extract
2 packages (9 ounces *each*) yellow cake mix

Pour pie filling into a greased 13-in. x 9-in. x 2-in. baking dish. Bake at 350° for 5-7 minutes or until heated through. Meanwhile, in a mixing bowl, cream butter, cream cheese and vanilla. Place cake mixes in another bowl; cut in butter mixture until crumbly. Sprinkle over hot filling. Bake 25-30 minutes longer or until topping is golden brown. **Yield:** 12 servings.

Orange Cobbler

Margery Bryan, Royal City, Washington

For a deliciously different dessert with two servings, try this mouth-watering cobbler. It's perfect for when I'm cooking for just the two of us and not a crowd. The orange marmalade is a sweet and tangy base.

>   2 tablespoons sugar
>   1 tablespoon cornstarch
> 1/2 cup cold water
> 1/4 cup orange marmalade
>   2 tablespoons orange juice concentrate
>   2 teaspoons butter *or* margarine
> 1/2 cup biscuit/baking mix
> Dash ground nutmeg
>   3 tablespoons milk
> Vanilla ice cream

In a saucepan, combine sugar and cornstarch. Stir in water, marmalade and orange juice concentrate. Cook and stir over medium-low heat until thickened. Stir in the butter until melted. Pour into a greased 1-qt. baking dish. In a bowl, combine biscuit mix and nutmeg; stir in milk just until moistened. Drop by tablespoonfuls over orange mixture. Bake, uncovered, at 400° for 20-25 minutes or until topping is golden brown. Serve warm with ice cream. **Yield:** 2 servings.

Macaroon Apple Cobbler

Phyllis Hinck, Lake City, Minnesota
(Pictured below)

Especially when I'm just serving a dessert, I like to prepare this comforting and crowd-pleasing cobbler. I'll usually make it with fresh apples—but I've also sometimes used home-canned ones.

>   4 cups thinly sliced peeled tart apples
> 1/3 cup sugar
> 1/2 teaspoon ground cinnamon
> 1/2 cup flaked coconut
> 1/4 cup chopped pecans
> TOPPING:
> 1/2 cup butter *or* margarine, softened
> 1/2 cup sugar
>   1 egg
> 1/2 teaspoon vanilla extract
> 3/4 cup all-purpose flour
> 1/4 teaspoon baking powder

Place the apples in an ungreased 9-in. pie plate. In a small bowl, combine sugar and cinnamon; sprinkle over apples. Top with coconut and pecans; set aside. In a mixing bowl, cream butter and sugar. Add egg and vanilla; mix well. Combine flour and baking powder; add to the creamed mixture until blended. Carefully spread over apples. Bake at 350° for 25-30 minutes or until topping is golden brown and fruit is tender. Serve warm. **Yield:** 6-8 servings.

Grape Pear Crisp

Donna Mosher, Augusta, Montana

You'll be pleasantly surprised by this unusual fruit combination. Over the years, we have enjoyed this dessert topped with whipped cream or ice cream. In fact, I've worn out the recipe card several times.

> 1-1/2 cups halved seedless grapes
>   1 can (16 ounces) sliced pears, drained
>   2 tablespoons plus 1/2 cup all-purpose flour, *divided*
> 1/4 teaspoon almond extract
> 1/3 cup packed brown sugar
> 1/2 teaspoon salt
> 1/4 teaspoon ground cinnamon
> 1/4 teaspoon ground nutmeg
> 1/4 cup cold butter *or* margarine
> 1/2 cup finely chopped walnuts

In a bowl, combine the grapes, pears, 2 tablespoons flour and extract until blended. Spoon into a lightly greased 8-in. square baking dish. In another bowl, combine brown sugar, salt, cinnamon, nutmeg and remaining flour; cut in butter until mixture resembles coarse crumbs. Stir in walnuts; sprinkle over fruit. Bake at 375° for 30 minutes or until lightly browned. **Yield:** 6-8 servings.

Raspberry Crisp

Donna Craik, Ladysmith, British Columbia

I grow raspberries, so I'm always thrilled to find new ways to use the fruit. But one "old" way that my family loves raspberries is in this crisp, which is my mom's recipe. I think of her every time I serve it.

    4 cups fresh raspberries, *divided*
    3/4 cup sugar
    2 tablespoons cornstarch
    1-3/4 cups quick-cooking oats
    1 cup all-purpose flour
    1 cup packed brown sugar
    1/2 teaspoon baking soda
    1/2 cup cold butter *or* margarine
Whipped cream

Crush 1 cup raspberries; add enough water to measure 1 cup. In a saucepan, combine sugar and cornstarch; stir in raspberry mixture. Bring to a boil; cook and stir for 2 minutes or until thickened. Remove from the heat; stir in the remaining raspberries. Cool. In a bowl, combine the oats, flour, brown sugar and baking soda. Cut in butter until mixture resembles coarse crumbs. Press half of the crumbs into a greased 9-in. square baking dish. Spread with cooled berry mixture. Sprinkle with remaining crumbs. Bake at 350° for 25-30 minutes or until topping is lightly browned. Serve warm with whipped cream. **Yield:** 8 servings.

Pear Crisp

Joanne Korevaar, Burgessville, Ontario

(Pictured below)

Since he's a livestock truck driver, my husband often starts work around 2 or 3 a.m. A piece of this crisp will keep him going until breakfast.

    8 medium ripe pears, peeled and thinly sliced
    1/4 cup orange juice
    1/2 cup sugar
    1 teaspoon ground cinnamon
    1/4 teaspoon ground allspice
    1/4 teaspoon ground ginger
TOPPING:
    1 cup all-purpose flour
    1 cup old-fashioned oats

    1/2 cup packed brown sugar
    1/2 teaspoon baking powder
    1/2 cup cold butter *or* margarine
Fresh mint and additional pear slices, optional

Toss pears with orange juice; place in a greased 13-in. x 9-in. x 2-in. baking dish. In a small bowl, combine the sugar, cinnamon, allspice and ginger; sprinkle over the pears. In a bowl, combine flour, oats, brown sugar and baking powder; cut in butter until crumbly. Sprinkle over pears. Bake at 350° for 35-40 minutes or until topping is golden brown and fruit is tender. Serve warm. Garnish with mint and additional pear slices if desired. **Yield:** 12 servings.

Date Pudding Cobbler

Carolyn Miller, Guys Mills, Pennsylvania

(Pictured above)

There were eight children in my family when I was a girl, and all of us enjoyed this cobbler. I now serve it for everyday and special occasions alike, and it's always well received. It's a tangy change of pace from the more traditional fruit cobblers.

    1 cup all-purpose flour
    1-1/2 cups packed brown sugar, *divided*
    2 teaspoons baking powder
    1 tablespoon cold butter *or* margarine
    1/2 cup milk
    3/4 cup chopped dates
    3/4 cup chopped walnuts
    1 cup water
Whipped cream and ground cinnamon, optional

In a bowl, combine flour, 1/2 cup brown sugar and baking powder. Cut in butter until crumbly. Gradually add milk, dates and walnuts. In a saucepan, combine water and remaining brown sugar; bring to a boil. Remove from the heat; add the date mixture and mix well. Transfer to a greased 8-in. square baking pan. Bake at 350° for 30 minutes or until golden brown. If desired, top each serving with a dollop of whipped cream and sprinkling of cinnamon. **Yield:** 9 servings.

George Washington Cherry Cobbler

Juanita Sherwood, Charleston, Illinois

(Pictured above)

We lived on a farm with lots of fruit trees when I was growing up, and since my father loved fruit, my mom prepared it often in many different ways, including using it in this pleasing cobbler. Blackberries or blueberries can also be used in place of the cherries.

1/2 cup sugar
2 tablespoons cornstarch
1/4 teaspoon ground cinnamon
3/4 cup water
1 package (12 ounces) frozen dark sweet cherries, thawed
1 tablespoon butter *or* margarine
TOPPING:
1 cup all-purpose flour
4 tablespoons sugar, *divided*
2 teaspoons baking powder
1/2 teaspoon salt
3 tablespoons shortening
1/2 cup milk
Ice cream, optional

In a saucepan, combine sugar, cornstarch and cinnamon. Stir in water until smooth. Add the cherries and butter. Bring to a boil over medium heat, stirring frequently. Cook and stir for 2 minutes or until thickened. Pour into an 8-in. square baking pan; set aside. In a bowl, combine flour, 2 tablespoons sugar, baking powder and salt. Cut in shortening until mixture resembles coarse crumbs. Stir in milk just until moistened. Drop by spoonfuls over the cherries; sprinkle with remaining sugar. Bake at 400° for 30-35 minutes or until golden brown. Serve warm with ice cream if desired. **Yield:** 8 servings.

Berry Apple Crumble

Ginger Isham, Williston, Vermont

(Pictured below and on p. 88)

You can serve this fruit crumble as a snack, but it's also great for a breakfast gathering or church supper. It is good served hot out of the oven. If there are any leftovers, it's good on the second day as well. The nutty topping is sweetened with Vermont maple syrup.

8 to 10 tart apples, peeled and sliced
2 tablespoons cornstarch
1 can (12 ounces) frozen apple juice concentrate, thawed
2 tablespoons butter *or* margarine
1 teaspoon ground cinnamon
1 teaspoon lemon juice
1 cup fresh *or* frozen blackberries
1 cup fresh *or* frozen raspberries
TOPPING:
2 cups quick-cooking oats
1/2 cup all-purpose flour
1/2 cup chopped walnuts
1/3 cup vegetable oil
1/3 cup maple syrup

Place the apples in a greased 13-in. x 9-in. x 2-in. baking dish; set aside. In a large saucepan, combine cornstarch and apple juice concentrate until smooth. Bring to a boil; cook and stir for 2 minutes or until thickened. Stir in the butter, cinnamon and lemon juice until butter is melted. Pour over the apples. Sprinkle with berries. In a bowl, combine the oats, flour and walnuts; add oil and syrup. Sprinkle over berries. Bake at 350° for 40-45 minutes or until topping is golden brown and filling is bubbly. **Yield:** 10-12 servings.

Chocolate Cobbler

Margaret McNeil, Memphis, Tennessee

It's impossible to resist the flavorful chocolate sauce that appears when this delightful dessert bakes.

> 1 cup self-rising flour*
> 1/2 cup sugar
> 2 tablespoons plus 1/4 cup baking cocoa, *divided*
> 1/2 cup milk
> 3 tablespoons vegetable oil
> 1 cup packed brown sugar
> 1-3/4 cups hot water
> Vanilla ice cream, optional

In a bowl, combine the flour, sugar and 2 tablespoons cocoa. Stir in milk and oil until smooth. Pour into a greased 8-in. square baking pan. Combine the brown sugar and remaining cocoa; sprinkle over batter. Pour hot water over top (do not stir). Bake at 350° for 40-45 minutes or until top of cake springs back when lightly touched. Serve warm with ice cream if desired. **Yield:** 6-8 servings. ***Editor's Note:** As a substitute for self-rising flour, place 1-1/2 teaspoons baking powder and 1/2 teaspoon salt in a measuring cup. Add all-purpose flour to measure 1 cup.

Almond Rhubarb Cobbler

Pat Habiger, Spearville, Kansas

(Pictured at right)

In spring, I often make this tangy biscuit-topped treat for my family, much to their delight.

> 1 cup sugar, *divided*
> 1/2 cup water
> 6 cups chopped rhubarb
> 2 tablespoons all-purpose flour
> 2 tablespoons butter *or* margarine
> 1/2 cup slivered almonds, toasted
> TOPPING:
> 1 cup all-purpose flour
> 2 tablespoons sugar
> 1-1/2 teaspoons baking powder
> 1/4 teaspoon salt
> 1/4 cup cold butter *or* margarine
> 1 egg
> 1/4 cup milk

In a large saucepan, bring 1/2 cup sugar and water to a boil. Add the rhubarb. Reduce heat; cover and simmer until tender, about 5 minutes. Combine flour and remaining sugar; stir into rhubarb mixture. Return to a boil; cook and stir for 2 minutes or until thickened and bubbly. Stir in butter and almonds. Reduce heat to low; stir occasionally. In a bowl, combine the dry ingredients; cut in butter until crumbly. Whisk egg and milk; stir into crumb mixture just until moistened. Pour hot rhubarb mixture into a greased shallow 2-qt. baking dish. Drop

topping into six mounds over the rhubarb mixture. Bake, uncovered, at 400° for 20-25 minutes or until golden brown. Serve warm. **Yield:** 6 servings.

Cherry Pineapple Crisp

Annabell Jordan, Broken Arrow, Oklahoma

I made this crisp for our children when they were growing up. Now our grandkids love it as well. Cherries and pineapple are a tasty combination.

> 2 cans (16 ounces *each*) pitted tart cherries
> 1 can (20 ounces) crushed pineapple, undrained
> 1 cup sugar
> 1/3 cup quick-cooking tapioca
> 2 cups all-purpose flour
> 1 cup packed brown sugar
> 3/4 cup quick-cooking oats
> 1 teaspoon baking powder
> 1/2 teaspoon salt
> 1-1/2 teaspoons vanilla extract
> 3/4 cup cold butter *or* margarine
> Ice cream, optional

Drain cherries, reserving 1/3 cup juice. Place cherries and reserved juice in a saucepan; add pineapple, sugar and tapioca. Let stand for 15 minutes. Meanwhile, in a bowl, combine flour, brown sugar, oats, baking powder and salt. Add vanilla; toss. Cut in butter until crumbly; press half into a greased 13-in. x 9-in. x 2-in. baking dish. Bring cherry mixture to a boil, stirring occasionally; cook and stir for 1 minute or until thickened and bubbly. Pour over crust. Sprinkle with remaining oat mixture. Bake at 375° for 25-30 minutes or until topping is golden brown and filling is bubbly. Serve warm with ice cream if desired. **Yield:** 12 servings.

Black and Blue Cobbler

Martha Creveling, Orlando, Florida

(Pictured below and on p. 88)

It never occurred to me that I could bake a fruit cobbler in my slow cooker until I saw some recipes and decided to try my favorite fruity dessert recipe. It took a bit of experimenting, but everyone agrees the tasty results are "berry" well worth it.

 1 cup all-purpose flour
1-1/2 cups sugar, *divided*
 1 teaspoon baking powder
 1/4 teaspoon salt
 1/4 teaspoon ground cinnamon
 1/4 teaspoon ground nutmeg
 2 eggs, beaten
 2 tablespoons milk
 2 tablespoons vegetable oil
 2 cups fresh *or* frozen blackberries
 2 cups fresh *or* frozen blueberries
 3/4 cup water
 1 teaspoon grated orange peel
Whipped cream *or* ice cream, optional

In a bowl, combine flour, 3/4 cup sugar, baking powder, salt, cinnamon and nutmeg. Combine eggs, milk and oil; stir into dry ingredients just until moistened. Spread the batter evenly onto the bottom of a greased 5-qt. slow cooker. In a saucepan, combine blackberries, blueberries, water, orange peel and remaining sugar; bring to a boil. Remove from the heat; immediately pour over batter. Cover and cook on high for 2 to 2-1/2 hours or until a toothpick inserted into the batter comes out clean. Turn slow cooker off. Uncover and let stand for 30 minutes before serving. Serve with whipped cream or ice cream if desired. **Yield:** 6 servings.

Applescotch Crisp

Elaine Nicholl, Nottingham, Pennsylvania

Just as soon as the first crop of apples is off the trees, I fix this crisp. Thanks to the butterscotch pudding, it's moist and sweet. It's popular at potlucks and is also a nice snack. In fact, I'm reluctant to make it in the evening—I'm afraid someone will sneak down to the refrigerator at midnight and claim it!

 4 cups sliced peeled tart apples
 1/2 cup packed brown sugar
 1 tablespoon plus 2/3 cup all-purpose flour, *divided*
 1/2 cup water
 1/4 cup milk
 1/2 cup quick-cooking oats
 1 package (3.5 ounces) cook-and-serve butterscotch pudding mix
 1/4 cup sugar
 1 teaspoon ground cinnamon
 1/2 teaspoon salt
 1/2 cup cold butter *or* margarine
Ice cream, optional

Place the apples in an ungreased 11-in. x 7-in. x 2-in. baking dish. In a bowl, whisk brown sugar, 1 tablespoon flour, water and milk. Pour over apples. In another bowl, combine oats, pudding mix, sugar, cinnamon, salt and the remaining flour. Cut in butter until mixture resembles coarse crumbs. Sprinkle over apples. Bake at 350° for 45-50 minutes or until topping is golden brown and fruit is tender. Serve with ice cream if desired. **Yield:** 8 servings.

Apricot Cobbler

Shirley Leister, West Chester, Pennsylvania

Call it old-fashioned, comforting or mouth-watering—all those descriptions fit this down-home dessert. It bakes up golden brown with a crunchy topping.

 3/4 cup sugar
 1 tablespoon cornstarch
 1/4 teaspoon ground cinnamon
 1/8 teaspoon ground nutmeg
 1 cup water
 3 cans (15-1/4 ounces *each*) apricot halves, drained
 1 tablespoon butter *or* margarine
TOPPING:
 1 cup all-purpose flour
 1 tablespoon sugar
1-1/2 teaspoons baking powder
 1/2 teaspoon salt
 3 tablespoons cold butter *or* margarine
 1/2 cup milk

In a saucepan, combine sugar, cornstarch, cinnamon and nutmeg. Stir in water until smooth; bring to a boil

over medium heat. Boil and stir for 1 minute; reduce heat. Add apricots and butter; heat through. Pour into a greased 2-qt. baking dish. For topping, combine flour, sugar, baking powder and salt in a bowl; cut in butter until crumbly. Stir in milk just until moistened. Spoon over hot apricot mixture. Bake at 400° for 30-35 minutes or until golden brown and a toothpick inserted into the topping comes out clean. **Yield:** 6 servings.

Sweet Potato Cobbler

Sherry Parker, Jacksonville, Alabama

(Pictured above and on p. 88)

My grandmother used to make the best sweet potato cobbler, but, like many cooks, she didn't follow a recipe. I tried many cobbler recipes before I discovered this one. It's a favorite for church dinners and is a special treat at home.

       2 pounds sweet potatoes, peeled and sliced
          1/4 inch thick
  3-1/2 cups water
  1-1/2 cups sugar
       3 tablespoons all-purpose flour
  1/2 teaspoon ground cinnamon
  1/4 teaspoon salt
  1/4 teaspoon ground nutmeg
  3/4 cup butter *or* margarine, cubed
PASTRY:
       2 cups all-purpose flour
  1/2 teaspoon salt
  2/3 cup shortening
       5 to 6 tablespoons cold water
       2 tablespoons butter *or* margarine, melted
       4 teaspoons sugar
Whipped cream, optional

In a saucepan, cook sweet potatoes in water until crisp-tender, about 10 minutes. Drain, reserving 1-1/2 cups cooking liquid. Layer potatoes in a greased 13-in. x 9-in. x 2-in. baking dish; add reserved liquid. Combine sugar, flour, cinnamon, salt and nutmeg; sprinkle over potatoes. Dot with butter. For pastry, combine flour and salt; cut in shortening until mixture resembles coarse crumbs. Gradually add water, tossing with a fork until a ball forms. On a floured surface, roll pastry into a 13-in. x 9-in. rectangle. Place over filling; cut slits in top.

Brush with butter; sprinkle with sugar. Bake at 400° for 30-35 minutes or until top is golden brown. Spoon into dishes; top with whipped cream if desired. **Yield:** 10-12 servings.

Almond Plum Kuchen

Norma Enders, Edmonton, Alberta

(Pictured below)

You'll find this dessert both easy and very tasty. Everyone who tries it comments on how the orange and plum flavors go together so well and complement each other. We like it best when it is served warm with ice cream.

  1-1/2 cups all-purpose flour
  3/4 cup packed brown sugar
  1/2 cup ground almonds
       1 tablespoon grated orange peel
  3/4 cup cold butter *or* margarine
FILLING:
       3 eggs
  3/4 cup sugar
  1/2 cup all-purpose flour
  1/2 cup ground almonds
       1 tablespoon grated orange peel
  1/2 teaspoon baking powder
       7 to 8 cups quartered fresh plums
TOPPING:
  1/4 cup sugar
  1/4 cup all-purpose flour
  1/4 cup butter *or* margarine, softened
  1/2 cup sliced almonds

In a bowl, combine the first four ingredients; cut in butter until the mixture resembles coarse crumbs. Press into a greased 13-in. x 9-in. x 2-in. baking dish. Bake at 375° for 15 minutes. Meanwhile, in a mixing bowl, beat eggs and sugar until thick and lemon-colored, about 5 minutes. Stir in flour, almonds, orange peel and baking powder. Arrange plums over crust; pour egg mixture over plums. Combine the first three topping ingredients; sprinkle over filling. Top with almonds. Bake for 40-45 minutes or until golden brown. **Yield:** 12 servings.

ABC Slump

Becky Burch, Marceline, Missouri

(Pictured above)

The "ABC" in this recipe's name comes from the apple, blueberries and cranberries it uses. The other part refers to the way the dumplings "slump" during cooking—presumably the sound made by the fruit as it bubbles on the stove. I've taken my slump to work, picnics and church carry-ins. No matter where, the result is the same…all that I ever bring home is the empty dish.

    1 cup chopped peeled tart apple
    1 cup fresh *or* frozen blueberries
  3/4 cup fresh *or* frozen cranberries
    1 cup water
  2/3 cup sugar
DUMPLINGS:
  3/4 cup all-purpose flour
  1/4 cup sugar
    1 teaspoon baking powder
  1/4 teaspoon ground cinnamon
  1/8 teaspoon ground nutmeg
    3 tablespoons cold butter *or* margarine
  1/3 cup milk
Half-and-half cream, optional

In a 3-qt. saucepan, combine the fruit, water and sugar; bring to a boil. Reduce heat; cover and simmer for 5 minutes. Meanwhile, in a bowl, combine the flour, sugar, baking powder, cinnamon and nutmeg; cut in butter until mixture resembles coarse crumbs. Add milk; stir just until moistened. Drop into six mounds onto simmering fruit. Cover and simmer for about 10 minutes or until a toothpick inserted into a dumpling comes out clean (do not lift the cover while simmering). Serve warm with cream if desired. **Yield:** 6 servings.

Rhubarb Granola Crisp

Arlene Beitz, Cambridge, Ontario

When my husband and I moved to our house in town after living in the country for so many years, the rhubarb patch had to come along! This crisp featuring that tangy fruit is a hit whether I serve it warm with ice cream on top or cold.

    4 cups chopped fresh *or* frozen rhubarb,
      thawed and drained
1-1/4 cups all-purpose flour, *divided*
  1/4 cup sugar
  1/2 cup strawberry jam
1-1/2 cups granola cereal
  1/2 cup packed brown sugar
  1/2 cup chopped pecans
  1/2 teaspoon ground cinnamon
  1/2 teaspoon ground ginger
  1/2 cup cold butter *or* margarine
Ice cream, optional

In a bowl, combine the rhubarb, 1/4 cup flour and sugar; stir in jam and set aside. In another bowl, combine the granola, brown sugar, pecans, cinnamon, ginger and remaining flour. Cut in butter until the mixture resembles coarse crumbs. Press 2 cups of the granola mixture into a greased 8-in. square baking dish; spread rhubarb mixture over the crust. Sprinkle with remaining granola mixture. Bake at 375° for 30-40 minutes or until topping is golden brown and filling is bubbly. Serve warm with ice cream if desired. **Yield:** 9 servings.

Blackberry Cobbler

Tina Hankins, Laconia, New Hampshire

(Pictured below)

Fresh blackberries abound in fields and alongside country roads in late summer around here. My whole fami-

ly thinks it's fun to pick them, especially when we know this fruity dessert will be the result. It's a treat we look forward to every season.

1/4 cup butter *or* **margarine, softened**
1/2 cup sugar
1 cup all-purpose flour
2 teaspoons baking powder
1/2 cup milk
2 cups fresh *or* **frozen blackberries**
3/4 cup raspberry *or* **apple juice**
Ice cream *or* **whipped cream, optional**

In a mixing bowl, cream butter and sugar. In another bowl, combine the flour and baking powder; add to the creamed mixture alternately with milk. Stir just until moistened. Pour into a greased 1-1/2-qt. baking dish. Sprinkle with blackberries. Pour juice over all. Bake at 350° for 45-50 minutes or until golden brown. Serve warm; top with ice cream or whipped cream if desired. **Yield:** 6-8 servings.

Caramel Apricot Grunt

Shari Dore, Brantford, Ontario

(Pictured on p. 88)

The "guinea pig" for my cooking is my husband. But this recipe is one we enjoyed at my grandmother's house. It's perfect for dessert or church socials.

2 cans (15-1/4 ounces *each***) apricot halves, undrained**
2 teaspoons quick-cooking tapioca
1/3 cup packed brown sugar
1 tablespoon butter *or* **margarine**
1 tablespoon lemon juice
DUMPLINGS:
1-1/2 cups all-purpose flour
1/2 cup sugar
2 teaspoons baking powder
2 tablespoons cold butter *or* **margarine**
1/2 cup milk
TOPPING:
1/4 cup packed brown sugar
2 tablespoons water
Half-and-half cream, optional

In a saucepan, combine apricots and tapioca; let stand for 15 minutes. Add brown sugar, butter and lemon juice. Cook and stir until mixture comes to a full boil. Reduce heat to low; keep warm. For dumplings, combine flour, sugar and baking powder in a bowl; cut in butter until crumbly. Add milk; mix just until combined. Pour warm fruit mixture into an ungreased 2-qt. baking dish (mixture will be very thick). Drop the batter into six mounds onto fruit mixture. Cover and bake at 425° for 15 minutes or until a toothpick inserted into a dumpling comes out clean (do not lift the cover while baking). In a saucepan, bring brown sugar and water to a boil; cook until sugar is dissolved. Spoon over dumplings; bake, uncovered, 5 minutes longer. Serve with cream if desired. **Yield:** 6 servings.

Magic Pumpkin Buckle

Darlene Markel, Stayton, Oregon

(Pictured above)

Probably my family's favorite pumpkin dessert, this is something I've been making since our two grown daughters were small. The crust mixture, which is actually poured in first, rises to the top during baking to form a rich topping.

1/2 cup butter *or* **margarine, melted**
1 cup all-purpose flour
1 cup sugar
4 teaspoons baking powder
1/2 teaspoon salt
1 cup milk
1 teaspoon vanilla extract
FILLING:
3 cups cooked *or* **canned pumpkin**
1 cup evaporated milk
2 eggs
1 cup sugar
1/2 cup packed brown sugar
1 tablespoon all-purpose flour
1 teaspoon ground cinnamon
1/2 teaspoon salt
1/4 teaspoon *each* **ground ginger, cloves and nutmeg**
TOPPING:
1 tablespoon butter *or* **margarine**
2 tablespoons sugar

Pour butter into a 13-in. x 9-in. x 2-in. baking dish; set aside. In a bowl, combine the flour, sugar, baking powder and salt. Stir in milk and vanilla until smooth. Pour into the prepared pan. In a mixing bowl, beat the pumpkin, milk and eggs. Combine the remaining filling ingredients; add to pumpkin mixture. Pour over crust mixture (do not stir). Dot with butter and sprinkle with sugar. Bake at 350° for 55-60 minutes or until a knife inserted near the center comes out clean and the top is golden brown. **Yield:** 12 servings.

p. 108

p. 103

p. 104

p. 108

p. 108

Tempting Tarts

PRETTY PASTRIES. Clocwise from upper left: Vanilla Cream Fruit Tart (p. 108), Autumn Apple Tart (p. 104), White Chocolate Fruit Tart (p. 103), Cherry Almond Tart (p. 108) and Pistachio Pudding Tarts (p. 108).

Heavenly Blueberry Tart

Lyin Schramm, Berwick, Maine

(Pictured above)

Mmm—this tart is bursting with the fresh flavor of blueberries! Not only do I bake the berries on the crust, but, after I take the tart out of the oven, I top it with just-picked fruit.

    1 cup all-purpose flour
    2 tablespoons sugar
    1/8 teaspoon salt
    1/2 cup cold butter *or* margarine
    1 tablespoon vinegar
FILLING:
    2 pints fresh blueberries, *divided*
    2/3 cup sugar
    2 tablespoons all-purpose flour
    1/2 teaspoon ground cinnamon
    1/8 teaspoon ground nutmeg

In a bowl, combine flour, sugar and salt; cut in butter until crumbly. Gently mix in vinegar to moisten. Press onto the bottom and up the sides of a lightly greased 9-in. tart pan with a removable bottom. Place 1 pint of blueberries over crust. Combine sugar, flour, cinnamon and nutmeg; sprinkle over blueberries. Bake at 400° for 55-60 minutes or until crust is browned and filling is bubbly. Remove from the oven; arrange and press remaining berries in a single layer over top. Cool on a wire rack. **Yield:** 6-8 servings.

Tiny Shortbread Tarts

Kim Marie Van Rheenen, Mendota, Illinois

(Pictured at right)

These tasty little tarts are nice for a family—kids love having their own tiny pies. For company, I use a vari-

ety of pie fillings and arrange the eye-pleasing tarts on a pretty platter.

    1 cup butter *or* margarine, softened
    1/2 cup confectioners' sugar
    2 cups all-purpose flour
    1 can (21 ounces) raspberry, cherry *or* strawberry pie filling

In a mixing bowl, cream butter and confectioners' sugar. Add flour; mix well. Shape into 1-in. balls; press onto the bottom and up the sides of greased miniature muffin cups. Bake at 300° for 17-22 minutes. Cool for 15 minutes; carefully remove from pans. Spoon 1 teaspoon of pie filling into each tart. **Yield:** about 3 dozen.

Sweet Butter Tarts

Charlene Turnbull, Wainwright, Alberta

A friend of mine first introduced me to this easy recipe. I usually whip up six or eight batches at Christmastime to give as gifts.

Pastry for three single-crust pies
    1/4 cup butter *or* margarine, softened
    1 cup packed brown sugar
    1 egg
    2 tablespoons milk
    1 teaspoon vanilla extract
    1/4 teaspoon maple flavoring
    1/2 cup raisins

Roll out pastry on a lightly floured surface; cut into twelve 4-in. circles. Press onto the bottom and up the sides of greased muffin cups. In a small mixing bowl, cream the butter and brown sugar. Add egg, milk, vanilla and maple flavoring. Stir in raisins. Fill each cup half full. Bake at 375° for 25 minutes or until crust is golden brown. **Yield:** 1 dozen.

Rhubarb Crumb Tart

Rebecca Gairns, Prince George, British Columbia

This is a favorite with my family, but especially my brother. He declares it "the most awesome dessert he's ever tasted"!

    1 cup all-purpose flour
    1 teaspoon baking powder
    3 tablespoons confectioners' sugar
    1/3 cup cold butter *or* margarine
    1 egg, beaten
    4 teaspoons milk
FILLING:
    3 cups diced fresh rhubarb
    1 package (3 ounces) strawberry gelatin
TOPPING:
    1/2 cup all-purpose flour
    1 cup sugar
    1/3 cup cold butter *or* margarine

In a bowl, combine flour, baking powder and confectioners' sugar; cut in butter until mixture resembles coarse crumbs. Add egg and milk; stir until a ball forms. Pat into a greased 11-in. x 7-in. x 2-in. baking dish. Place rhubarb in crust. Sprinkle gelatin over rhubarb. In a small bowl, combine flour and sugar; cut in butter until crumbly. Sprinkle over rhubarb mixture. Bake at 350° for 45-50 minutes. Cool completely before cutting. **Yield:** 12-15 servings.

Reheating Fruit Tarts

Add that just-baked touch by reheating fruit-filled tarts and pies in a 300° oven for 10 to 15 minutes.

White Chocolate Fruit Tart

Claire Darby, New Castle, Delaware

(Pictured above and on p. 100)

It takes a little time to make, but this tart is absolutely marvelous, especially in summer.

    3/4 cup butter *or* margarine, softened
    1/2 cup confectioners' sugar
  1-1/2 cups all-purpose flour
FILLING:
    1 package (10 ounces) vanilla *or* white chips, melted
    1/4 cup whipping cream
    1 package (8 ounces) cream cheese, softened
    1 can (20 ounces) pineapple chunks, undrained
    1 pint fresh strawberries, sliced
    1 can (11 ounces) mandarin oranges, drained
    2 kiwifruit, peeled and sliced
GLAZE:
    3 tablespoons sugar
    2 teaspoons cornstarch
    1/2 teaspoon lemon juice

In a mixing bowl, cream butter and sugar. Gradually beat in flour. Press into an ungreased 11-in. tart pan or 12-in. pizza pan with sides. Bake at 300° for 25-30 minutes or until lightly browned. Cool. In a mixing bowl, beat chips and cream. Beat in cream cheese until smooth. Spread over crust. Chill for 30 minutes. Drain pineapple, reserving 1/2 cup juice. Arrange the fruits over filling. In a saucepan, combine sugar, cornstarch, lemon juice and reserved pineapple juice; bring to a boil over medium heat. Cook and stir for 2 minutes or until thickened. Cool; brush over fruit. Chill 1 hour before serving. **Yield:** 12-16 servings.

Autumn Apple Tart

Michele Bentley, Waukesha, Wisconsin

(Pictured below and on p. 100)

There are so many apple orchards in our state, and this tasty tart is one of my favorite ways to use this abundant fall fruit.

CRUST:
1-1/4 cups all-purpose flour
1 teaspoon baking powder
1/2 teaspoon salt
1 tablespoon sugar
1/2 cup cold butter *or* margarine
1 egg, beaten
2 tablespoons milk
6 medium tart apples, peeled, cored and sliced 1/4 inch thick
TOPPING:
1/3 to 1/2 cup sugar
1-1/2 tablespoons all-purpose flour
1/2 teaspoon ground cinnamon
1/2 teaspoon ground nutmeg
2 tablespoons cold butter *or* margarine

In a bowl, combine flour, baking powder, salt and sugar; cut in butter until mixture resembles fine crumbs. Combine egg and milk; add to crumb mixture. Stir to blend. With lightly floured hands, press dough onto the bottom and 1 in. up the sides of a 12-in. tart pan with removable bottom or 13-in. x 9-in. x 2-in. baking pan. Fill tart shell with overlapping apple slices, beginning at outer edge. For topping, combine the sugar, flour, cinnamon and nutmeg; cut in butter until crumbly. Sprinkle evenly over apples. Bake at 350° for 50-60 minutes or until apples are tender. **Yield:** 12 servings.

Apricot Tarts

Phyllis Hickey, Bedford, New Hampshire

(Pictured above)

These tiny apricot-filled tarts are an extra-special dessert for any holiday or occasion. We love the fruity and nutty flavor.

1/2 cup butter *or* margarine, softened
1 package (3 ounces) cream cheese, softened
1 cup all-purpose flour
3/4 cup finely chopped dried apricots
3/4 cup water
1/3 cup chopped pecans
1/4 cup sugar
2 tablespoons orange marmalade
1/2 teaspoon ground cinnamon
1/8 teaspoon ground cloves
TOPPING:
2 tablespoons cream cheese, softened
1 tablespoon butter *or* margarine, softened
1/2 teaspoon vanilla extract
1/2 cup confectioners' sugar

In a mixing bowl, beat butter, cream cheese and flour until blended. Chill for 1 hour. Meanwhile, in a saucepan, bring the apricots and water to a boil. Reduce heat; simmer for 5 minutes. Drain. Add the pecans, sugar, marmalade, cinnamon and cloves; set aside. Shape dough into 24 balls. Press onto the bottom and up the sides of greased miniature muffin cups. Spoon apricot mixture into cups. Bake at 350° for 25-30 minutes or until browned. Cool for 10 minutes; remove from pans to wire racks to cool completely. For topping, combine cream cheese and butter in a small mixing bowl. Stir in vanilla until smooth. Beat in confectioners' sugar. Spoon a dollop onto each tart just before serving. **Yield:** 2 dozen.

Miniature Almond Tarts

Karen Van Den Berge, Holland, Michigan

My family requests these adorable little tarts each Christmas. I always enjoy making them since the almond paste in the filling reflects our Dutch heritage, plus they're popular at special gatherings.

CRUST:
1 cup butter *or* margarine, softened
2 packages (3 ounces *each*) cream cheese, softened
2 cups all-purpose flour
FILLING:
6 ounces almond paste, crumbled
2 eggs, beaten
1/2 cup sugar
FROSTING:
1-1/2 cups confectioners' sugar
3 tablespoons butter *or* margarine, softened
4 to 5 teaspoons milk
Maraschino cherry halves (about 48)

In a small mixing bowl, cream the butter and cream cheese. Add flour; mix well. Cover and refrigerate for 1 hour. Shape into 1-in. balls. Press onto the bottom and up the sides of ungreased miniature muffin cups. For filling, combine the almond paste, eggs and sugar in a small mixing bowl. Beat on low speed until blended. Fill each shell with about 1-1/2 teaspoons filling. Bake at 325° for 25-30 minutes or until edges are golden brown. Cool for 10 minutes before removing from pans to wire racks to cool completely. For frosting, combine the confectioners' sugar, butter and enough milk to achieve desired consistency. Pipe or spread over tarts. Top each with a cherry half. Store in the refrigerator. **Yield:** about 4 dozen.

Sour Cream Tarts

Crystal Fogelsanger, Newville, Pennsylvania

This last-minute dessert is delicious, especially with cherry pie filling on top. But just about any pie filling flavor tastes fantastic. For even quicker assembly, use a prepared 9-inch graham cracker crust.

1-1/2 cups cold milk
1 package (5.1 ounces) instant vanilla pudding mix
2 cups (16 ounces) sour cream
2 packages (6 count *each*) individual graham cracker tart shells
1 can (21 ounces) fruit pie filling

In a mixing bowl, beat milk and pudding mix on low speed for 2 minutes. Fold in sour cream. Spoon about 1/3 cup into each tart shell; top with pie filling. Serve immediately. **Yield:** 12 servings.

Peaches 'n' Cream Tart

Mary Ann Kosmas, Minneapolis, Minnesota
(Pictured below)

You'll find this luscious dessert as easy as it is elegant. You can bake the crust ahead—then it's mostly a matter of whipping together the filling.

1 cup finely chopped pecans
2/3 cup all-purpose flour
1/2 cup butter *or* margarine, melted
1/2 cup whipping cream
1 package (8 ounces) cream cheese, softened
1/3 cup sugar
1 teaspoon vanilla extract
1/2 teaspoon almond extract
1 teaspoon grated orange peel
1 can (15-1/4 ounces) sliced peaches, drained
1/2 cup fresh raspberries
1/4 cup apricot preserves
2 tablespoons honey

Combine pecans, flour and butter; press onto the bottom and up the sides of an ungreased 9-in. tart pan with removable bottom. Bake at 350° for 25-30 minutes or until golden brown. Cool completely. Whip cream until soft peaks form; set aside. In a mixing bowl, beat the cream cheese and sugar until fluffy. Add extracts and orange peel; mix well. Beat in the whipped cream on low speed. Spoon into crust. Chill for 2-4 hours. Just before serving, arrange peaches and raspberries over filling. In the microwave, melt preserves and honey; stir until blended. Carefully spoon or brush over fruit. Cut into wedges to serve. **Yield:** 6-8 servings.

Good Glaze Ideas

Glaze tarts or single-crust fruit pies by lightly brushing the surface with warm, light corn syrup 10 minutes after removing from the oven.

Depending on the fruit's flavor, you could also use melted currant or apple jelly with just as equally delicious results.

Fresh Blueberry Tarts

Pat Habiger, Spearville, Kansas

These attractive individual treats deliver a burst of blueberry flavor that's unbeatable. I appreciate their quick and easy convenience on those days I don't have much time to put together supper—let alone dessert—for my hungry family.

    1 package (8 ounces) cream cheese, softened
1/4 cup packed light brown sugar
    1 package (6 count) individual graham
        cracker tart shells
    2 cups fresh blueberries, *divided*
    3 tablespoons sugar
    1 teaspoon lemon juice
    1 teaspoon grated lemon peel

In small mixing bowl, beat cream cheese and brown sugar until smooth. Spoon into the tart shells. In a bowl, mash 3 tablespoons blueberries with sugar, lemon juice and peel. Stir in the remaining berries and toss to coat. Spoon over filling. Chill for 1 hour before serving. **Yield:** 6 servings.

Peanut Butter Tarts

Sheryl Christian, Watertown, Wisconsin

I feel it's important for my family to sit down and have a meal together at least once a day. These cool and creamy tarts are the perfect peanutty finale to many of our meals. I keep the ingredients on hand for quick snacks, too.

    1 carton (8 ounces) frozen whipped topping,
        thawed
10 to 12 individual graham cracker tart shells
    1 cup cold milk
2/3 cup creamy peanut butter
    1 package (3.4 ounces) instant vanilla
        pudding mix
    2 tablespoons jelly (flavor of your choice)

Spoon a tablespoonful of whipped topping into the bottom of each tart shell; set aside. In a mixing bowl, beat milk and peanut butter until well blended. Add pudding mix and beat for 1 minute. Fold in the remaining whipped topping. Spoon about 1/2 cup of the filling into each tart shell. Chill. Just before serving, top each with 1/2 teaspoon jelly. Leftovers may be frozen. **Yield:** 10-12 servings.

Pecan Tarts

Jean Rhodes, Tignall, Georgia

(Pictured below)

The flaky crust combined with a rich center makes these little tarts a satisfying snack to serve and eat. They look so appealing on a pretty platter and make a great finger-food dessert when you're entertaining. They also freeze well.

    1 package (3 ounces) cream cheese,
        softened
1/2 cup butter *or* margarine, softened
    1 cup all-purpose flour
1/4 teaspoon salt
FILLING:
    1 egg
3/4 cup packed dark brown sugar
    1 tablespoon butter *or* margarine, melted
    1 teaspoon vanilla extract
2/3 cup chopped pecans
Maraschino cherry halves, optional

In a mixing bowl, beat cream cheese and butter; blend in flour and salt. Chill for 1 hour. Shape into 1-in. balls; press onto the bottom and up the sides of greased miniature muffin cups. For filling, beat the egg in a small mixing bowl. Add brown sugar, butter and vanilla; mix well. Stir in pecans. Spoon into tart shells. Bake at 325° for 25-30 minutes. Cool in pans on wire racks. Decorate with maraschino cherry halves if desired. **Yield:** about 20.

Almond Pear Tartlets

Marie Rizzio, Traverse City, Michigan

(Pictured above)

Although they're quick to fix, you'll want to savor these pretty pastries slowly. Delicately spiced pears are complemented by a chilled almond sauce and a crispy puff pastry crust. Be prepared to share the recipe. I've had many requests over the years.

　　1 egg, lightly beaten
　1/2 cup plus 6 tablespoons sugar, *divided*
　　3/4 cup whipping cream
　　2 tablespoons butter *or* margarine, melted
　1/2 teaspoon almond extract
　　1 package (10 ounces) frozen puff pastry
　　　shells, thawed
　　2 small ripe pears, peeled and thinly sliced
　1/2 teaspoon ground cinnamon
　1/8 teaspoon ground ginger
　1/2 cup slivered almonds, toasted, optional

In a small saucepan, combine the egg, 1/2 cup sugar, whipping cream and butter. Cook and stir until the sauce is thickened and a thermometer reads 160°. Remove from the heat; stir in almond extract. Cover and refrigerate. Meanwhile, on an unfloured surface, roll out each puff pastry into a 4-in. circle. Place in an ungreased 15-in. x 10-in. x 1-in. baking pan. Top each pastry circle with pear slices. Combine the cinnamon, ginger and remaining sugar; sprinkle over pears. Bake at 400° for 20 minutes or until pastry is golden brown. Sprinkle with almonds if desired. Serve warm with the chilled cream sauce. **Yield:** 6 servings.

Apple Cranberry Tart

Jo Ann Fisher, Huntington Beach, California

(Pictured below)

People practically inhale this dessert. I modified another recipe years ago to come up with a different way of using cranberries—a favorite fruit of mine.

1-1/4 cups unsweetened apple juice *or* cider,
　　　divided
1-1/3 cups sugar
　　3 medium tart apples, peeled and cubed
　　1 package (12 ounces) fresh *or* frozen
　　　cranberries
　1/2 cup all-purpose flour
Pastry for single-crust pie (10 inches)
TOPPING:
　1/3 cup chopped pecans
　1/3 cup all-purpose flour
　　3 tablespoons butter *or* margarine, melted
　1/4 cup packed brown sugar
　12 pecan halves

In a saucepan over medium heat, bring 3/4 cup apple juice and sugar to a boil, stirring occasionally. Add apples and cranberries; return to a boil. Reduce heat; simmer, uncovered, until apples are tender and berries pop, about 5-8 minutes. Whisk flour and remaining juice until smooth; stir into cranberry mixture. Bring to a boil; cook and stir for 2 minutes. Cool to room temperature. Fit pastry into an 11-in. fluted tart pan with removable bottom, or press onto the bottom and 1 in. up the sides of a 10-in. springform pan. Line pastry with double thickness of heavy-duty foil. Bake at 450° for 5 minutes. Remove foil; bake 7-10 minutes longer or until pastry is lightly browned. Cool. Add apple mixture. Combine first four topping ingredients; sprinkle over filling. Arrange pecan halves on top. Bake at 375° for 30-35 minutes or until golden brown. **Yield:** 12 servings.

Vanilla Cream Fruit Tart

Susan Terzakis, Andover, Massachusetts

(Pictured above and on p. 100)

It's well worth the effort to prepare this spectacular tart, which is best made and served the same day. A friend gave me the recipe, and it always receives rave reviews at gatherings.

```
  3/4 cup butter or margarine, softened
  1/2 cup confectioners' sugar
1-1/2 cups all-purpose flour
    1 package (10 ounces) vanilla or white chips,
      melted and cooled
  1/4 cup whipping cream
    1 package (8 ounces) cream cheese,
      softened
    1 pint fresh strawberries, sliced
    1 cup fresh blueberries
    1 cup fresh raspberries
  1/4 cup sugar
    1 tablespoon cornstarch
  1/2 cup pineapple juice
  1/2 teaspoon lemon juice
```

In a mixing bowl, cream butter and confectioners' sugar. Beat in flour (mixture will be crumbly). Pat into a greased 12-in. pizza pan. Bake at 300° for 25-28 minutes or until lightly browned. Cool. In another mixing bowl, beat melted chips and whipping cream. Add cream cheese; beat until smooth. Spread over crust. Chill for 30 minutes. Arrange strawberries, blueberries and raspberries over filling. In a saucepan, combine sugar, cornstarch, pineapple juice and lemon juice; bring to a boil over medium heat. Cook and stir for 2 minutes or until thickened. Cool; brush over the top of the fruit. Chill 1 hour before serving. Store leftovers in the refrigerator. **Yield:** 12-16 servings.

Cherry Almond Tart

Connie Raterink, Caiedonia, Michigan

(Pictured on p. 100)

I use on-hand ingredients to create this dazzling dessert. It's fast to fix, looks elegant and tastes delicious.

```
  1 package (18-1/4 ounces) yellow cake mix
2/3 cup graham cracker crumbs (about 11
      squares)
1/2 cup butter or margarine, softened
  1 egg
1/2 cup chopped almonds
  1 package (8 ounces) cream cheese,
      softened
1/4 cup confectioners' sugar
  1 can (21 ounces) cherry pie filling
1/2 cup sliced almonds, toasted
```

In a mixing bowl, combine the dry cake mix, cracker crumbs and butter until crumbly. Add egg; mix well. Stir in the chopped almonds. Press onto the bottom and up the sides of a greased 14-in. pizza pan. Bake at 350° for 11-13 minutes or until lightly browned. Cool completely. In a mixing bowl, beat cream cheese and sugar. Spread over crust. Top with pie filling. Sprinkle with sliced almonds. Store leftovers in the refrigerator. **Yield:** 14-16 servings.

Pistachio Pudding Tarts

Bettye Linster, Atlanta, Georgia

(Pictured on p. 100)

For St. Patrick's Day, Christmas or anytime you want a treat that's green, refreshing and delightful, try these tempting little tarts.

1 cup butter *or* margarine, softened
1 package (8 ounces) cream cheese, softened
2 cups all-purpose flour
1-3/4 cups cold milk
1 package (3.4 ounces) instant pistachio pudding mix

In a mixing bowl, combine butter, cream cheese and flour; mix well. Shape into 48 balls; press onto the bottom and up the sides of ungreased miniature muffin cups. Bake at 400° for 12-15 minutes or until lightly browned. Cool for 5 minutes; carefully remove from pans to wire racks to cool completely. For filling, combine milk and pudding in a mixing bowl; beat on low speed for 2 minutes. Cover and refrigerate for 5 minutes. Spoon into tart shells; serve immediately. **Yield:** 4 dozen.

Brownie Tarts

Sharon Wilkins, Grande Pointe, Ontario

(Pictured below)

I often take these bite-size chocolate goodies to potluck dinners for our country dance club.

1/2 cup butter *or* margarine, softened
1 package (3 ounces) cream cheese, softened
1 cup all-purpose flour
FILLING:
1/2 cup semisweet chocolate chips
2 tablespoons butter *or* margarine
1/2 cup sugar
1 egg, beaten
1 teaspoon vanilla extract
1/2 cup chopped pecans, optional
Maraschino cherry halves, optional

In a mixing bowl, cream the butter and cream cheese. Add flour; mix well. Chill for 1 hour. Shape into 1-in. balls. Place in ungreased miniature muffin cups; press onto the bottom and up the sides to form a shell. For filling,

melt chocolate chips and butter in a small saucepan. Remove from the heat; stir in sugar, egg and vanilla. Add the pecans if desired. Spoon into shells. Bake at 325° for 30-35 minutes or until brownies test done with a toothpick. Cool for 10 minutes before removing to wire racks. Garnish with cherries if desired. **Yield:** 2 dozen.

Walnut Tart

Rovena Wallace, Trafford, Pennsylvania

(Pictured above)

The first time my husband tried this, he said there ought to be a law against anything tasting so good! I've served it at picnics and family occasions…and even once at a bridal shower.

1/3 cup butter *or* margarine, softened
1/4 cup sugar
1 egg yolk
1 cup all-purpose flour
FILLING:
2 cups coarsely chopped walnuts
2/3 cup packed brown sugar
1/4 cup butter *or* margarine
1/4 cup dark corn syrup
1/2 cup whipping cream, *divided*

In a mixing bowl, cream butter and sugar until fluffy. Add egg yolk; mix well. Add flour just until blended (mixture will be crumbly). Press onto the bottom and up the sides of an ungreased 9-in. tart pan with removable bottom. Bake at 375° for 12-14 minutes. Cool in the pan on a wire rack. Sprinkle nuts over crust. In a heavy saucepan, combine brown sugar, butter, corn syrup and 2 tablespoons of cream. Bring to a boil over medium heat; cook and stir for 1 minute. Pour over walnuts. Bake at 375° for 10-12 minutes or until bubbly. Cool. Beat remaining cream until stiff. Serve with whipped cream. **Yield:** 10-12 servings. **Editor's Note:** An 11-in. x 7-in. x 2-in. baking pan may be used instead of a tart pan.

INDEX

This handy index lists each recipe by major ingredients. For specific types of pies, refer to the recipe list at the beginning of each chapter.

Index